What Life Was Like

AT THE DAWN OF DEMOCRACY

Classical Athens
525 – 322 BC

What Life Was Like

AT THE DAWN OF DEMOCRACY

Classical Athens
525 - 322 BC

BY THE EDITORS OF TIME-LIFE BOOKS, ALEXANDRIA, VIRGINIA

CONTENTS

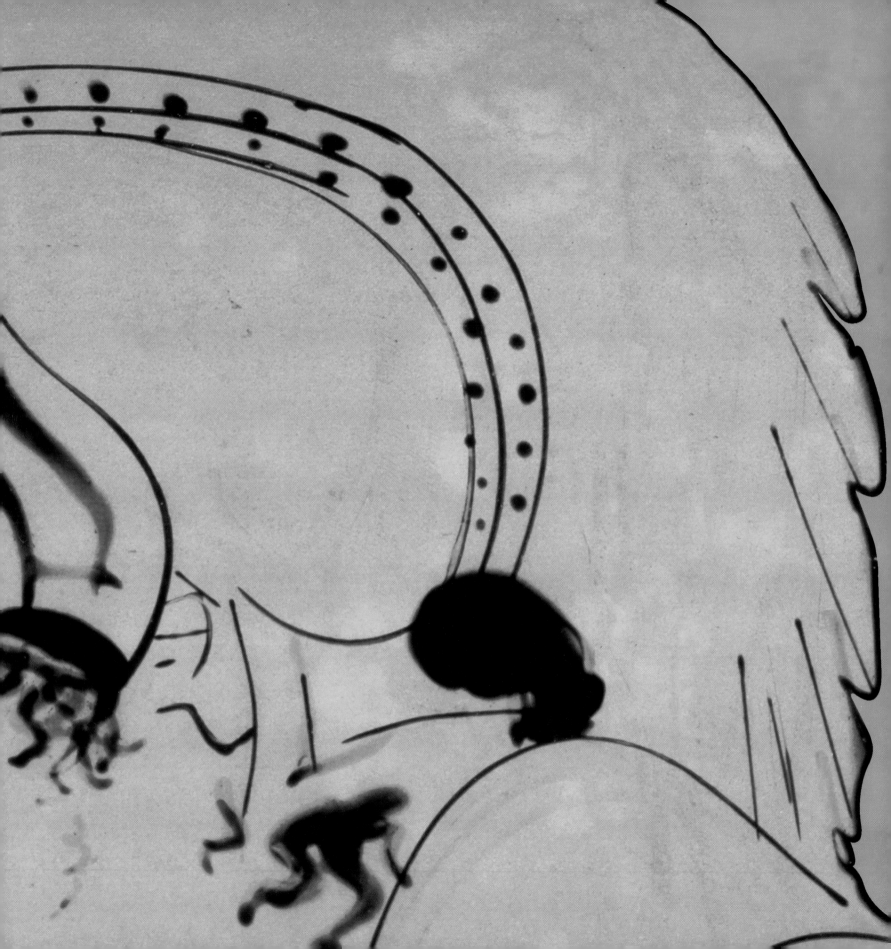

AT THE DAWN
OF DEMOCRACY

THE GREEK WORLD

When Athena, goddess of wisdom and war, and the sea god, Poseidon, were competing for possession of one of the cities of ancient Greece, the other gods decreed that the city should be awarded to the one who bestowed upon its inhabitants the most useful gift. In response, Poseidon struck the ground with his trident and brought forth a miraculous saltwater spring. Athena, putting her faith in a more practical offering, planted an olive tree beside the spring. The people found the olive a better gift, and the city was named for its winner: Athens.

The rise of Athens began during the time known as the Mycenaean Age. From about 1600 BC the Mycenaean culture flourished in several parts of mainland Greece, including Thebes, Argos, and Athens, as well as in the city of Mycenae, from which it took its name. Eventually the power of the Mycenaeans eclipsed the civilization of Minoan Crete, which had dominated the Aegean Sea from around the 20th century BC.

The Mycenaeans borrowed much from the Minoans. Like their predecessors, they lived in what are known as palace cultures, societies that revolved around huge stone-palace complexes whose kings made laws and governed the economy. But unlike the Minoans, the Mycenaeans were mighty warriors, and Greek mythology abounds with stories of their exploits.

It was during this time that the Trojan War was said to have taken place. According to the eighth-century poet Homer, who preserved their legendary deeds forever, Agamemnon, Achilles, Odysseus, and the other heroes of Mycenaean Greece fought 10 long years for the return of a stolen princess, Helen. But while they battled "windy Troy," trouble was stirring at home. And finally, between 1250 and 1190 BC, the culture suffered a cataclysmic collapse that was probably brought on by revolution, civil war, invasion, famine, or some combination of these forces. The Mycenaean government vanished, most of the great palace centers were destroyed or abandoned, and many of the survivors migrated across the Aegean to settle the islands and coasts of Asia Minor.

Little is known about this period; hence its name, the Dark Age. Poverty seems to have been widespread, and most Greek

Height of the Minoan civilization	The Mycenaean Age	Greeks begin colonization of the coast of Asia Minor	First Olympic Games are held	Hoplite armor developed; Athens unites with the other towns of Attica; Greek alphabet created; Greek colonies are established in Italy; Homer composes *Iliad* and *Odyssey*	Draco writes first code of laws
2200-1500 BC	1600-1200 BC	ca. 1100 BC	ca. 776 BC	750-700 BC	621 BC

communities were ruled by petty lords who, guarding their independence, acknowledged only reluctantly any form of central control. Over time these local loyalties began to coalesce into larger communities, and by the eighth century BC the Greek world had evolved into a collection of independent states. Each *polis*, as the states were known, consisted of a city and the lands around it, and most were less than 100 square miles in area. The people of each polis possessed a distinct cultural identity. But they worshiped gods that belonged to the same basic pantheon, they spoke a common language, and the introduction of an alphabet from the Near East soon after 750 facilitated communication among the groups.

At this time, most city-states were oligarchies, governed by aristocratic landowners. As overseas trade increased in the seventh century, though, the new wealth often went to men who were outside the ruling classes; predictably, these rich merchants, craftsmen, and bankers came to resent their lack of political influence. Rioting often resulted, and from around the year 650 powerful individual leaders began to challenge the old ways. These men were known as tyrants, although the term carried with it none of our modern connotations of cruelty and oppression; exploiting popular discontent with the ruling elites, they tried to seize power for themselves.

Such was the case in Athens and its surrounding territory of Attica, the largest of the Greek city-states and, with as many as 350,000 inhabitants, the most populous. A peninsula measuring no more than 50 miles across, Attica was sheltered from its rivals by a barrier of mountains to the north and by the Aegean Sea in other directions. Yet the Aegean also acted as a channel of communication, drawing to Athens a constant flow of people and ideas along with the trade that helped make the city prosper.

As in the rest of Greece, the aristocrats were firmly entrenched in Athens, serving as its chief officials, or *archontes,* and dominating its council. But about 632 a former Olympic champion tried to overthrow the city's unpopular rulers and set himself up as tyrant. The coup failed, and according to tradition, in 621 a lawmaker named Draco drew up a set of penal codes. Draco specified death as the penalty for most crimes, giving rise to the term *draconian.* When asked about the harshness of his code, Draco allegedly replied that small crimes deserved death and that he could not think of a greater penalty for large crimes.

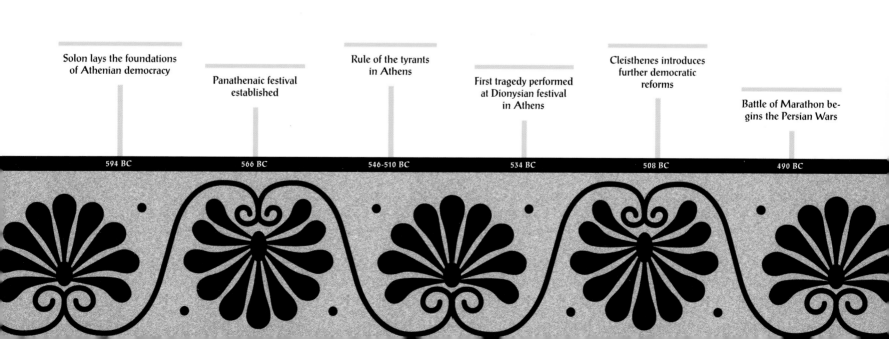

Solon lays the foundations of Athenian democracy

Panathenaic festival established

Rule of the tyrants in Athens

First tragedy performed at Dionysian festival in Athens

Cleisthenes introduces further democratic reforms

Battle of Marathon begins the Persian Wars

594 BC   566 BC   546-510 BC   534 BC   508 BC   490 BC

In 594 an aristocratic archon named Solon repealed most of Draco's laws and began to introduce reforms. Solon's laws permitted nonaristocrats to hold administrative positions. He set up a people's council, or boule, to rival that of the aristocrats, and it was probably during this time that an assembly of the Athenian people began to meet. Despite the reforms, anarchy broke out again, and around 546 a military leader by the name of Peisistratus seized power. His rule was largely a success, and he appears to have been popular. Under his direction Athens enjoyed a period of peace and prosperity.

When Peisistratus died in 527 his son Hippias became tyrant. Hippias ruled until 510, when he was overthrown. Two years of civil war followed, at the end of which a reformer named Cleisthenes introduced political measures that opened membership of the assembly to all adult male citizens, regardless of income or class. But by the beginning of the fifth century another threat to the developing Athenian democracy was looming: the growing empire of Persia. The Persians had already annexed the Greek city-states of Asia Minor, and in 490 a Persian war fleet sailed for the shores of mainland Greece.

During this crisis, known as the Persian Wars, the city-states were able to set aside their differences and band together to resist the invaders. They scored great victories over the Persians, as at Marathon, but suffered humiliating reverses, too. The Persians captured Athens, for example, and burned shrines and temples that had been built on the Acropolis, the sacred hill of Athena in the middle of the city.

Eventually the Greeks prevailed, and after the withdrawal of the Persians in 479, Athens entered its golden age. During these years Athenian ships plied the waters of the Mediterranean, taking the city's democratic philosophy to other Greek city-states, bringing the products of the world to its citizens, and, eventually, forging a maritime empire that embraced the whole Aegean. It was a time when tyrants and foreign invaders had been driven off, when the Athenian people and their assembly ruled supreme, a time when its foremost statesman, Pericles, could declare with confidence that Athens was "the school of Greece."

At Pericles' instigation a magnificent new temple was built on the Acropolis: the Parthenon, a majestic seat for Athena overlooking her own city. The Athens she would have seen was much

First ostracisms in Athens; first comedy performed at Dionysian festival in Athens

Birth of Hippocrates, founder of Western medicine

Work begins on the Parthenon

Herodotus, "the father of history," writes his nine-volume Histories

Statue of Athena by Phidias dedicated in Parthenon

The Peloponnesian War between Athens and Sparta

| 487 BC | 460 BC | 447 BC | 445-426 BC | 438 BC | 431-404 BC |

changed from the Mycenaean settlement for which she and Poseidon had supposedly competed. By the golden age it had developed into a great center for the arts that attracted the best dramatists, philosophers, sculptors, architects, and historians of the Greek world.

It was against this backdrop that the people of Athens played out their lives, lives that were ordered and ordained by their status in life: male or female, free man or slave, native-born citizen or foreign-born resident. Athens was a democracy—but one built on a social hierarchy, where only males could vote in the assembly, where slaves outnumbered citizens, and where many of the richest members of society—the resident aliens—were excluded completely from the political process.

And yet fifth-century Athens boasted the most progressive system of government that the world had ever seen and a society whose achievements would travel far beyond the shores of Greece. Ironically, the legacy of Athens would be passed on by its conquerors. After suffering defeat at the hands of Sparta in the closing years of the century, Athens fell under the shadow of its powerful northern neighbor, Macedonia, whose leader, Alexander the Great, spread Greek culture throughout his vast empire. And when, in the second century BC, Greece became part of Rome's empire, the Romans incorporated Athenian ideas and ideals into their own society, ensuring their inclusion in the foundation of modern Western civilization.

But during Greece's golden age, Athens had reigned supreme, a model city clustered around Athena's sacred mount, to be admired and emulated by the rest of Greece. In the chapters that follow we will meet some of the people who lived in Athens during that era. Some we will encounter as they walk through the city's marketplace, speak in its assembly, or work in its factories. We will see Athenians at leisure, participating in religious festivals, attending a theater performance, or spending an evening at one of the traditional banquets they called *symposia*. We will see the state's citizen-soldiers preparing for war, taking their place in battle formation or manning one of Athens's mighty triremes. As with other cultures, most daily life revolved around the home, and it is there that we will begin, taking a look inside the household of one Athenian family to discover a little of what life was like.

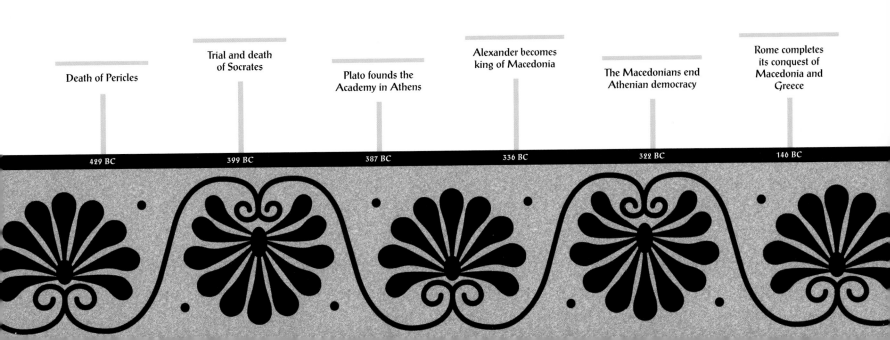

Death of Pericles	Trial and death of Socrates	Plato founds the Academy in Athens	Alexander becomes king of Macedonia	The Macedonians end Athenian democracy	Rome completes its conquest of Macedonia and Greece
429 BC	399 BC	387 BC	336 BC	322 BC	146 BC

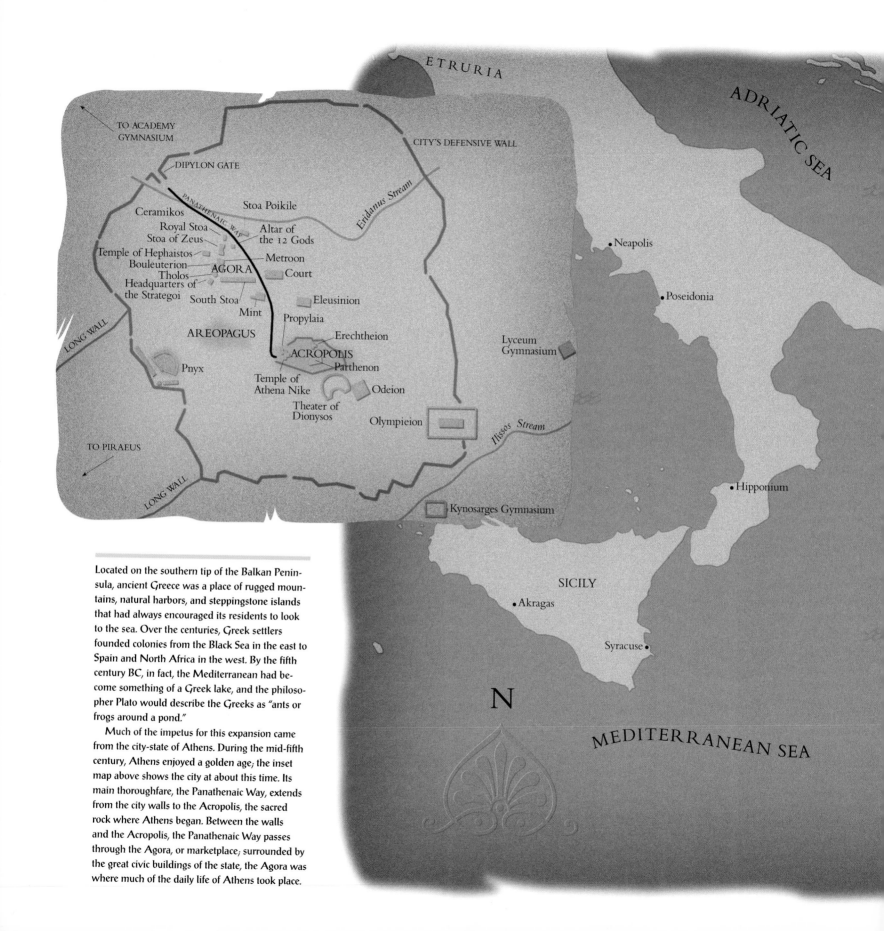

ETRURIA

ADRIATIC SEA

TO ACADEMY GYMNASIUM

CITY'S DEFENSIVE WALL

DIPYLON GATE

PANATHENAIC WAY

Stoa Poikile

Ceramikos

Royal Stoa
Stoa of Zeus

Altar of
the 12 Gods

Eridanus Stream

Temple of Hephaistos

Metroon

Bouleuterion

AGORA

Tholos

Court

Headquarters of
the Strategoi

South Stoa

Eleusinion

Mint

LONG WALL

AREOPAGUS

Propylaia

Erechtheion

Lyceum
Gymnasium

Pnyx

ACROPOLIS

Parthenon

Temple of
Athena Nike

Theater of
Dionysos

Odeion

TO PIRAEUS

Olympieion

Ilissos Stream

LONG WALL

Kynosarges Gymnasium

Neapolis

Poseidonia

Hipponium

SICILY

Akragas

Syracuse

N

MEDITERRANEAN SEA

Located on the southern tip of the Balkan Peninsula, ancient Greece was a place of rugged mountains, natural harbors, and steppingstone islands that had always encouraged its residents to look to the sea. Over the centuries, Greek settlers founded colonies from the Black Sea in the east to Spain and North Africa in the west. By the fifth century BC, in fact, the Mediterranean had become something of a Greek lake, and the philosopher Plato would describe the Greeks as "ants or frogs around a pond."

Much of the impetus for this expansion came from the city-state of Athens. During the mid-fifth century, Athens enjoyed a golden age; the inset map above shows the city at about this time. Its main thoroughfare, the Panathenaic Way, extends from the city walls to the Acropolis, the sacred rock where Athens began. Between the walls and the Acropolis, the Panathenaic Way passes through the Agora, or marketplace; surrounded by the great civic buildings of the state, the Agora was where much of the daily life of Athens took place.

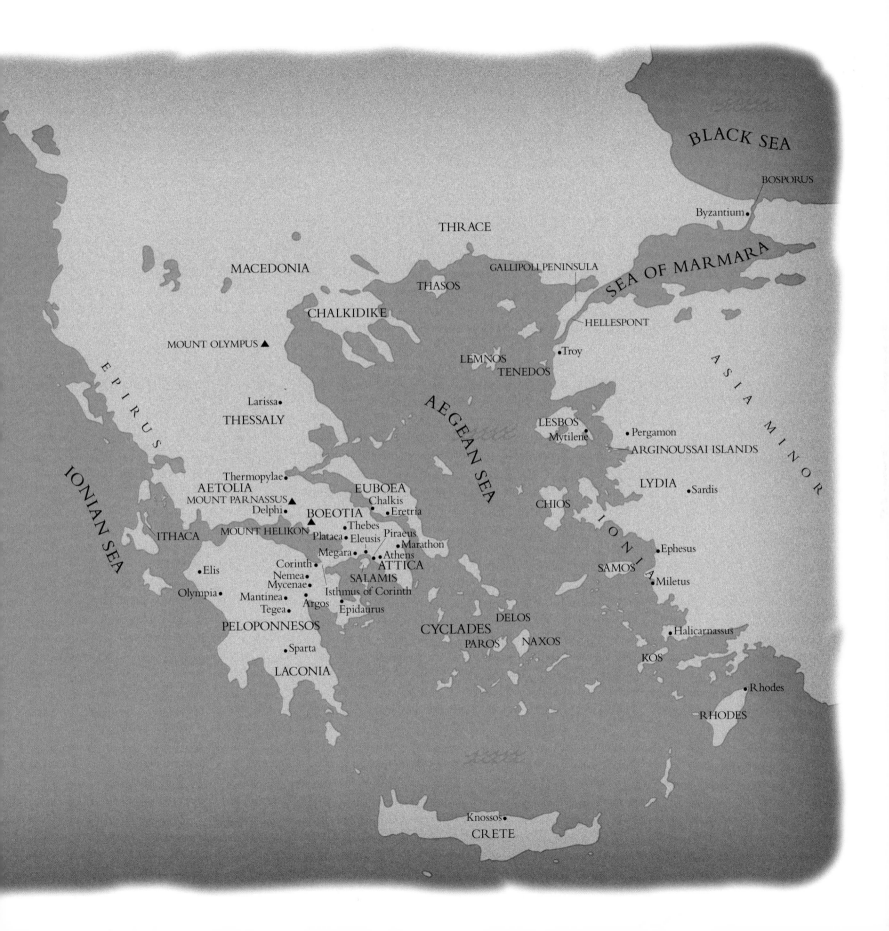

BLACK SEA

BOSPORUS

Byzantium

THRACE

MACEDONIA

SEA OF MARMARA

THASOS

GALLIPOLI PENINSULA

CHALKIDIKE

HELLESPONT

MOUNT OLYMPUS ▲

Troy

LEMNOS

TENEDOS

EPIRUS

Larissa

AEGEAN SEA

THESSALY

ASIA MINOR

LESBOS
Mytilene

Pergamon

ARGINOUSSAI ISLANDS

Thermopylae

IONIAN SEA

AETOLIA

EUBOEA

MOUNT PARNASSUS ▲

Chalkis

LYDIA

Delphi

Eretria

CHIOS

Sardis

BOEOTIA

▲

Piraeus

Thebes

IONIA

ITHACA

MOUNT HELIKON

Plataea

Eleusis

Marathon

Ephesus

Megara

Athens

Corinth

ATTICA

SAMOS

Elis

Nemea

Miletus

Mycenae

SALAMIS

Olympia

Mantinea

Isthmus of Corinth

Tegea

Argos

Epidaurus

Halicarnassus

PELOPONNESOS

CYCLADES

DELOS

KOS

Sparta

PAROS

NAXOS

LACONIA

Rhodes

RHODES

Knossos

CRETE

THE GODS OF OLYMPU

Although there was no centrally organized theology in ancient Greece, religious beliefs and rituals played a dominant role in daily life. The Greeks believed that their gods lived on the cloud-capped peak of snowy Mount Olympus in northern Thessaly *(far left)*. They also accepted the idea that these gods routinely meddled in the affairs of state and the lives of individuals, bringing both good and ill fortune. "For god often gives men a glimpse of happiness," observed the historian Herodotus, "only to ruin them root and branch." Besides the twelve major—or Olympian—gods, led by Zeus *(left),* the Greeks honored a host of lesser divinities and heroes. To maintain the goodwill of these deities they offered up prayers, sacrifices, and purification rituals. They also celebrated a multitude of religious festivals in honor of the gods—some involving all of Greece, others exclusive to a particular city-state.

Zeus and Mount Olympus, home of the gods

ZEUS AND HERA

To the Greeks, who relied on the land and sea for their livelihood, Zeus was the all-important god of the sky and weather. The poets Homer and Hesiod described him as the father of gods and mortals. While Zeus was first among the Olympians, he was not born into that position. He fought his way to the top by overthrowing his father, Kronos. In turn, tradition had it that Zeus—whose children included powerful gods as well as mortal heroes such as Herakles and Perseus—could be overthrown by a son destined to be more powerful than his father.

The Greeks built their largest temples and dedicated their most important festival, held every four years at Olympia, to Zeus. They honored Hera, Zeus's wife and sister, as the patron of weddings and marriage. The month of Gamelion—when Hera and Zeus were married—was the most popular time for weddings, and the families of both bride and groom would offer sacrifices to Hera and Zeus at the ceremony.

But Hera had a dark side that surfaced in her own marriage; Homer portrays her as the epitome of a jealous, vengeful spouse. Enraged by Zeus's many extramarital affairs, she persecuted his lovers, sometimes to death.

The god Zeus *(left)* and his wife, Hera *(right)*

Zeus took more than 100 divine and mortal women as lovers. At times he changed form to hide from Hera, as happened when he transformed himself into a bull and abducted Europa *(right)*. The jealous Hera often took revenge on her rivals. At her urging Semele *(below)* asked Zeus to reveal his full power and was consumed in the fire of his thunderbolt.

ATHENA, POSEIDON, AND HEPHAISTOS

Ancient Greece honored gray-eyed Athena both as goddess of wisdom and as patron of domestic arts. She also shared the patronage of crafts with the cunning blacksmith Hephaistos, god of fire, smiths, and artisans.

Like other Olympian gods, Athena, born of Zeus, had a ruthless side. Hesiod describes this goddess, often depicted as an armed maiden, as a "mistress who delights in the clamorous cry of war and battle and slaughter." Greeks believed that Athena sometimes came to the aid of her favorites on the battlefield, including Herakles and Odysseus. Athena, who was honored in her namesake city-state with a magnificent temple, won the patronage of Athens over Poseidon when her gift of an olive tree was chosen over Poseidon's offering of a spring of water.

Poseidon ruled the sea and was lord of horses. Greeks also attributed earthquakes and other natural disasters to this powerful brother of Zeus. Sailors offered Poseidon—guardian of fishermen and rescuer of ships—prayers before voyages. They also held chariot races and sacrificed bulls as well as horses to appease his wrath. In the *Odyssey*, Homer describes Poseidon's tempestuous reaction when he spied Odysseus, who had blinded the god's son Polyphemos: "Brewing high thunderheads, he churned the deep with both hands on his trident—called up wind from every quarter, and sent a wall of rain to blot out land and sea in torrential night."

The goddess Athena armed for war

With his double ax in hand, Hephaistos helps Athena emerge as she is born from Zeus's head.

Powerful Poseidon aims his trident.

APOLLO, ARTEMIS, ARES, AND APHRODITE

The ancient Greeks revered Apollo, the son of Zeus, as the god of inspiration. He had the power to bestow on men the gift of poetry, music, healing, or even the ability to act as his oracular go-between with other mortals. However, the arrows he shot from his bow could bring plague to men and animals alike. In a hymn Apollo summarizes his attributes: "May the dear lyre and the curved bow be mine, and I shall reveal too to men through my oracles the infallible designs of Zeus." Pilgrims from around the Greek world traveled to Apollo's famous oracle at Delphi. Contests were held to compose lyrics and verse in his honor; the winners were crowned with laurel wreaths, hence the title "poet laureate."

Apollo's sister, Artemis, was the goddess of the wilds and presided over the hunt. Often accompanied by dancing nymphs, she did not hesitate to shoot her deadly missiles at those who crossed her. She was also revered as the patroness of life's transitions. Her name was often invoked in rites of passage, such as those that marked children's leaving behind their world to assume a full-fledged role in society. A young woman would offer toys and other tokens of childhood to Artemis at a sacrifice held on the eve of her wedding.

Brides also offered sacrifices to Artemis's stepsister, Aphrodite, the goddess of love, who presided over sexuality and reproduction. Aphrodite possessed seductive charm and a penchant for deception, qualities attributed to women in general in Greece. But like the other Olympians she had a dual nature, and was worshiped in Athens as the goddess of civil harmony and protector of its citizens.

Apollo, the mighty bowman

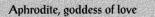

Aphrodite, goddess of love

In the *Iliad* Zeus says of the god of war, Ares, shown at left with his lover, Aphrodite: "You are the most hateful to me of all the gods who hold Olympus; forever strife is dear to you and wars and slaughter."

Hounds tear apart their master Aktaion, who glimpsed Artemis while she was bathing. In her anger she set his own dogs upon him.

HERMES, DEMETER, PERSEPHONE, AND HADES

Hermes served as the messenger of the Olympians, and he acted frequently as a go-between for Zeus. One of his important duties was to convey the souls of the dead to the underworld. Hermes was also depicted as a divine trickster: "Born at the dawning of the day, at midday he played on the lyre, and in the evening he stole the cattle of far-shooting Apollo." Hermes, who invented the lyre, eventually made amends with Apollo by giving him the instrument.

As goddess of agriculture, Demeter was much revered by the Greeks. According to the myth that explains the seasons and the cycles of vegetation, Hades, god of the underworld, spied Demeter's daughter, Persephone, gathering flowers and dragged her off to his home. Demeter searched the world for her daughter and finally, in her sorrow, took refuge in the territory of Eleusis. While she waited in seclusion for her daughter's return, "the earth sent up no seed, as fair-garlanded Demeter hid it." At Zeus's command, Hermes rescued Persephone and returned her to her mother. However, Persephone was compelled to go back to the underworld for a part of each year—winter. There she reigned as Hades' wife and queen.

Demeter and Persephone were honored by many festivals, including the Great Mysteries held in Eleusis at the end of summer. In wartime, a truce was called so that celebrants, who came from all over the Greek-speaking world, could travel safely to the festival. The six-day ritual began in Athens with a procession to Eleusis and ended with an assembly of the initiates and the unveiling of sacred objects. Since revelation of the rites was a capital offense, many details of these ceremonies remain a mystery.

Hermes, messenger of the gods

Lounging with a wine cup in hand, Hades shares a quiet moment with his wife, Persephone, who lived with him in the underworld for three months each year.

Demeter *(left)* and her symbol, a sheaf of grain

23

Wearing a crown of grape-
vines and ivy tendrils and a
panther skin around his
shoulders, Dionysos seems
dressed for a night of revels.

DIONYSOS AND HIS FOLLOWERS

A maenad, holding a wand wreathed in ivy, dances with her head lowered in a trance.

Dionysos was the son of Zeus and Semele, a mortal. In a jealous frenzy, Zeus's wife, Hera, pursued Dionysos and drove him mad. To the Greek people, Dionysos's madness represented a challenge to the natural order of things. The god of wine and intoxication, his worship included ritual madness and ecstasy. The Dionysian cult was one of the few social venues open to women, and they embraced their role wholeheartedly. In mountainous areas outside of Athens, female initiates called maenads abandoned their normal lives and ran across the mountain-tops, dancing wildly and ecstatically, possessed by the spirit of Dionysos and supposedly led by the god himself.

In Athens, the Athenians celebrated seven Dionysian festivals, among them a wine-drinking festival called the Anthesteria, which took place in early spring. On the first day of the festival, celebrants opened jars of new wine, which they mixed with water. Then, after pouring a libation to Dionysos, they sampled the new vintage. On the second day, processions reenacting Dionysian myths were followed by an evening of drinking at small gatherings. Unlike the custom at ordinary parties, however, guests brought their own food and wine to their host's house and drank in silence. On the eerie Halloween-like third day the Athenians, believing that evil spirits roamed the streets, offered sacrifices of food to the dead. That night, the head of every household banished ghosts from his dwelling by shouting, "Get out, evil spirits, the Anthesteria is over."

Satyrs, mythical servants of Dionysos with horses' tails, devote themselves to drink and merriment.

CHAPTER ONE

SCANDAL IN AN ATHENIAN HOUSEHOLD

A scene on a Greek vase portrays family members in their typical roles: The wife watches over her younger son; the husband carries a moneybag that shows that he provides for and controls his family; and, behind him, the older son stands near a strigil—used to scrape off sweat and dirt after sports—and sponge, which indicate that he is an athlete.

The city had long been asleep when Euphiletos, citizen of Athens, was roused unexpectedly from his rest. He had dined at home with a friend that evening and had dozed off soon after the man left. Now the servant who woke him had urgent news to impart.

The effect of her message was instantaneous and dramatic. Leaping from the couch on which he lay, Euphiletos pulled a calf-length woolen mantle over his tunic, grabbed his sandals, and padded quietly down the rickety wooden staircase of his home. Tiptoeing to the front door, he slipped on his footwear and went out of the house into the warm darkness of the unlit street.

Once outside, however, all sense of caution disappeared. Fired by his purpose, Euphiletos set off through the city's notoriously narrow alleys, here and there stopping at a house to hammer on the door and wake up the sleepers inside. Each time a startled face peered around the jamb, he would summon the head of the household to join him on his nocturnal mission. And before long a small, disheveled band of neighbors was following in his wake.

As he stalked ahead of them through the unpaved back streets, Euphiletos's mind was on the message that the servant had brought him

Houses in Athens were characterized by mud-brick walls; small, high windows; tiled roofs; and open courtyards. The men's rooms usually were on the ground floor, with the women's quarters upstairs.

went far beyond that, expanding to include past and future generations. Indeed, Athenian men liked to think of the oikos—the building block of the state and the producer of its citizens—as coming down to them by inheritance and extending before them toward the generations to come.

And the head of that household was invariably male. As the biographer Plutarch would later write, "In a virtuous household every activity is performed by husband and wife in agreement with each other, but it is nevertheless clear that it is the man who is in charge and has the power of decision." To a Greek man of the classical era, this point of view would have seemed uncontroversial, no more than a statement of the obvious. Accepting that responsibility was a man's allotted role.

This position of privilege enjoyed by Greek males was buttressed by law as well as by custom. For example, only men were permitted to own land, and Athenian legislators went to extraordinary lengths to ensure that, when a householder died, there was a legitimate male heir to succeed him. Hence, a widow was forced to put her estate under the protection of a son or other male guardian. And a father who had produced no male heir encouraged his daughter to marry an uncle or some other close relative in the hope of keeping

—the terrible tidings that an intruder was in his home. The enormity of it all got worse with every step. Not only the security of his home but also the moral integrity of his household was at risk, and to Greek males nothing mattered more than that institution. For the household—the *oikos*—was no mere abstract concept; rather, it was both a man's private sphere and his stake in the society in which he lived. Preserving it was not just an act of self-interest, it was a sacred duty.

To the ancient Greeks, the term *oikos* comprised both the house and the people who lived in it. Some parts of the household were obvious—such as a man's immediate family, the elderly parents for whom he was responsible, his domestic servants, and the house they all lived in. But the full meaning of *oikos*

Some Athenian women, mostly slaves or from the lower classes, were able to enjoy companionship at the public fountain, a place where they could fill their water jugs and meet and chat with neighbors.

To spin thread from wool or flax, Greek women used either a drop spindle *(below)* or the older method of rolling the fibers on the thigh while wearing an *epinetron (lower right),* a ceramic leg protector.

the estate within the family after his death. The legal system went further: In an effort to ensure that unions were productive, one Athenian law even specified that the couple must have intercourse a minimum of three times a month; failing that, the wife could turn to her husband's next of kin and could have him perform the expected marital duty.

The house, then, was just the physical representation of the private realm of the Athenian male. The core of the oikos was his wife; only she could provide him and his household with a link to the future generations through the birth of a son. Accordingly, the women's quarters—that part of the home reserved exclusively for the wife, daughters, and female domestics—were often on the second floor of the house, and thus most insulated from the street and the outside world. Only by isolating women in this way, it was believed, could males protect the virginity of unmarried girls and guarantee the fidelity of wives, so ensuring the legitimacy of future male heirs.

Any intrusion into this part of the house represented the worst violation of the oikos. And according to Euphiletos's servant, such an intrusion had just happened: A man had made his way into the room where Euphiletos's wife was sleeping; worse, the man was there at the invitation of Euphiletos's wife.

All that history has recorded of Euphiletos focuses on the events of that one traumatic night and the lawsuit that followed it. Consequently, much of the background that led him to his moment of truth can only be guessed at. But the pattern of life for Athenians of his class did not vary much, and from what we know

Two women weave on an upright
loom, working strands of yarn that
hang from an overhead beam and
are weighted at the bottom.

of others we can reconstruct with reasonable accuracy a picture of Euphiletos the Athenian.

Like his parents before him, Euphiletos almost certainly would have been born somewhere in the territory of Attica, where Athens was located, for during the late fifth century BC, when he lived, citizenship was restricted to those who were born to an Athenian father and an Athenian mother; only on rare occasions were outsiders granted the special privilege of citizenship. And although the available evidence is vague, Euphiletos seems to have been moderately well off: He had a house of his own, though not a particularly large one; and the trips that he took out to the countryside suggest that, like many Athenians, he also owned property beyond the city walls.

As a boy, Euphiletos would have been brought up by his mother for the first seven or eight years of his life. He would then have been transferred to the care of a *paidagogos,* a male servant who kept a watchful eye on his behavior and, if necessary, disciplined him by beating him with a strap or a cane. Among the servant's principal duties was to accompany his charge to and from classes each day.

Education in Athens was a private matter, but almost all citizens managed to find the money to provide their sons with at least a few years of schooling. Instruction came in three main subject areas. First, students would learn to read and write, scratching out letters with styluses on wax tablets and reciting passages from Homer and other poets that they were expected to learn by heart. Second, they participated in physical training, which was carried out in private gymnasia known as *palaistrai.* There boys practiced running, jumping, boxing, and wrestling, as well as javelin and discus throwing. And third, they learned music, which generally meant playing the lyre and the flute as well as singing. Although musical skills were regarded as less essential than the other two disciplines, the philosopher Aristotle warned against their neglect. "Those who train their children in

athletics to the exclusion of other necessities," he declared, "make their children truly vulgar."

It was often as a result of their time spent at the palaistrai that teenage boys gained yet another—unofficial—form of education. For it was there that they could be pursued by adult male admirers. According to the convention, it was considered to be socially acceptable for young, unmarried men to express longing for teenage boys and to court them with compliments as well as caresses; in return, the teenagers were expected to play a passive, subordinate role in the relationship. The attachment was not expected to last, however, ending either when the youth started growing a beard—and so losing his attraction—or when the admirer himself settled down and got married. Homosexual activity beyond that point was for the most part regarded with contempt.

But while they endured, such courtships were apparently carried out with much romantic passion. A character in Plato's dialogue the *Symposium,* for instance, talks of "everything that lovers do for the boys they cherish, the prayers and entreaties with which they support their suit, the oaths they swear, the nights they spend on the doorstep of the beloved one and the slavery they endure for his sake, which no real slave would put up with."

Ideally, the relationship was one based on pure affection, unswayed by the political power or wealth of the suitor. But often it developed into one of mentor and student, in which the older male took on the role of teacher and adviser, while the youth learned from his experience and his manly social and ethical qualities. In short, their association was frequently an exchange of beauty for moral wisdom and insight.

Such relationships in classical Greece never operated within fixed bounds, however. Nor were they universally approved. Strict legislation protected boys from unwanted attentions; sexual assault was considered a capital offense; and men could, in

In a famous scene from mythology, the bearded Zeus kidnaps the handsome youth Ganymede to serve as his personal cup-bearer on Mount Olympus.

SCHOOL DAYS

According to the philosopher Socrates, the three great concerns of an Athenian were the prosperity of his household, the chastity of his daughter, and the education of his son. Schooling began with a teacher known as a *grammatistes,* who would teach a boy only basic mathematics—probably little more than how to count with an abacus, with his "digits," or with pebbles. More important, the grammatistes taught his students to read, and

in particular to read—as well as recite from memory—sections from two epics, the *Iliad* and the *Odyssey.*

The cultural importance of these two great works of Homer—full of exciting tales and inspiring heroes—was also reflected in the lessons taught by a second teacher, the *kitharistes,* or lyre player. This instructor taught the boys to sing and play by using Homer's poetry, which was chanted to the accompaniment of the lyre. Training the

Students wrote on wax tablets with a stylus, like this one fashioned of ivory, using the blunt end to erase their mistakes.

In the scenes adorning the sides of this fifth-century-BC drinking cup, students receive instruction in playing the lyre, reading from a papyrus, singing to the aulos, or double flute, and writing on a wax tablet. Overseeing the activities are cane-wielding *paidagogoi,* family slaves charged with care of the young.

mind with literature and music was believed to improve a young man's soul, helping him form an upright character.

A boy's physical education fell to a third teacher, the *paidotribes,* who developed sound and healthy bodies. By the end of formal schooling, the three disciplines should have transformed a youth into a *kaloskagathos,* literally, "a beautiful and good man," the sort of gentleman of whom Athens could be proud.

Engaging in the only formal lessons she would receive, an Athenian maiden moves gracefully to a tune piped by her dance mistress on an aulos taken from the flute bag hanging on the wall. A girl's education usually was limited to domestic training—so that she might "see as little, hear as little, and ask as few questions as possible."

theory at least, be sentenced to death merely for entering a schoolroom without good reason. Further, the practice seems to have been limited largely to the better-off within society. When the comic playwright Aristophanes wanted to show that he had not been spoiled by success, he said jokingly that he hadn't taken to haunting the palaistrai—a trait that he evidently expected his audience to associate with the wealthy.

Whether the young Euphiletos had such a relationship with an older man we do not know. But we can assume that he would have stopped attending classes sometime in his midteens. After that age it was only the very rich who continued to educate their children, often sending them off to receive instruction from the so-called sophists, a

himself and his family from his country property. The next charted landmark in his career was when he made the fateful decision to get married.

Unfortunately, history has not preserved for us the name of Euphiletos's wife—a telling omission—but we will call her Demarete. She was most likely younger than Euphiletos, for girls tended to marry at about 14, often to men twice as old. At that tender age, Demarete's life already had been very different from that of the man her parents had chosen for her. As a child she would have received none of the formal schooling available to Euphiletos. Girls were educated at home, where they primarily learned housekeeping

"She was a clever housewife, economical and exact in her management of everything."

group of teachers, most of whom were foreign born, who offered training in rhetoric and philosophy.

Euphiletos's transition to manhood would have been marked by a ceremony in which his hair—allowed to grow long during childhood—was cut off and dedicated to one of the gods. And at 18 the young man was ready for two years of military service. During the first half of this service he would learn the art of war by developing an expertise in archery, javelin throwing, and fighting in heavy armor; and during the second half he would perform garrison duty on the frontiers of Attica. After that, his enlistment was over, although he remained liable to call-up in times of emergency until age 60.

By the age of 20 Euphiletos would finally have been ready to take his place among the ranks of Athenian citizens. What profession he chose to follow is unknown; perhaps he supported

skills, although some parents made sure that their daughters could read and write, and perhaps also dance and play the flute or lyre. But most probably she resembled the bride described by the historian Xenophon who at the time of her marriage knew "only how to take wool and produce a cloak, and had seen how spinning tasks are allocated to the slaves."

Demarete would have had little, if any, say in the choice of marriage partner, which may well have been decided by her parents long before she was of an age to have an opinion. A major consideration for any prospective groom would have been the size of the dowry that she took with her into the match; once she was married, the dowry would become her husband's to manage as he saw fit, although if the relationship subsequently broke down he would be obliged to return the money to her family.

But such thoughts must have been far from Demarete's mind

in the days before her wedding, a time of joy, nervousness—and probably more than a little fear. For during this transitional time, when both bride and groom were at the point of their life's fulfillment, they were deemed to be particularly vulnerable to the envy of the gods. And Demarete would have been all too familiar with the mythological tales of wedding disasters, tragedies in which the bride did not survive the transition from her old state to the new one.

To avoid such unfortunate occurrences, the prelude to Demarete's wedding would have been marked by sacrifices to the deities who blessed the marriage bed. For example, in order to complete a safe passage to the sphere of Aphrodite, goddess of sexual love, Demarete would have had to win the blessing of the goddess whose sphere she was leaving: Artemis, the virgin goddess and protector of children. Thus, on the day before her wedding Demarete might have dedicated her old toys and playthings to Artemis—as well as the virgin's girdle that she had been accustomed to wearing—thereby bidding farewell to her life as a child.

Then, using water from the one city fountain prescribed for the purpose, Demarete would have taken a ritual bath, figuratively cleansing herself of her maidenhood. Perhaps she looked again at her wedding clothes— her long veil and her crown, the heavy robe that would be tied with a loosely knotted cord—and shuddered at the great step that she was about to take.

Wealthy Greek women adorned themselves with jewelry such as the earrings this woman is fastening or the gold diadem with garnet at far right, both for status and to enhance their appeal to their husbands.

Demarete may have recalled that even the goddess Hera had undergone similar preparations before her union with Zeus, according to the poet Homer. In the *Iliad* the goddess bathes and anoints herself with oil, arranges her hair, and puts on an embroidered gown and a veil. Finally Hera persuades Aphrodite to lend her the belt that the latter wears over her bosom, imbued as it is with magical powers of seduction.

On the wedding day itself, Demarete would have waited until nightfall, as custom required, for Euphiletos to call at her family's home and formally claim her as his bride. This was probably the first time that the girl saw her husband-to-be. As she shyly peered out from behind her hand-held veil, she would probably have seen that Euphiletos was looking his best, too, in a finely woven cloak, wearing a garland on his head, and smelling of myrrh.

Then a procession would have formed to convey Demarete to her new home: This was the central act of the wedding. Bride and bridegroom mounted a wagon drawn by horses, mules, or oxen, with relatives and friends falling in behind on foot. With cries of "Get up!" "Make way!" and "Carry the torch!" the wagon and its followers started their slow procession.

During the torch-lit journey to Euphiletos's house the friends and family members sang the marriage hymn, to the accompaniment of flutes and lyres. Among the singers would have been Demarete's mother, who also carried one of the torches. But her torch was more than just a means of lighting the dark, narrow Athenian streets: The flame that she held aloft came from her hearth, symbolically protecting her daughter during the transition from one oikos and status to another. So integral were torches to the marriage ceremony, in fact, that one expression for an illegitimate union was "a wedding without torches."

When the procession reached Euphiletos's house—decorated with garlands made from olive and laurel leaves to mark it off as a festive space—the groom's parents and other relatives would be waiting to welcome Demarete. Particularly visible would have been Euphiletos's mother, who stood at the door to receive her daughter-in-law and held a torch ablaze with the fire of the girl's new home.

Entering the home, Euphiletos would lead Demarete to the hearth, its symbolic center, where the guests showered the newlyweds with fruits and nuts in celebration. There the bride was offered part of the wedding cake, traditionally made from sesame and honey, together with a quince or a date, both symbols of fertility. And by accepting this first food from her husband's house, Demarete would be binding herself to him.

From here the couple proceeded to the bridal chamber, where Demarete perhaps removed her veil for the first time. When the door closed behind them, a friend of the groom's would sit outside the newlyweds' room to prevent others from intruding, while the rest of the company sang nuptial hymns at the top of their voices in an effort to scare away evil spirits.

AN ATHENIAN WEDDING

A bridal party makes its way to the groom's house in a torch-lit procession in this illustration taken from a Greek perfume jar. The newly married couple, who may have met for the first time only that day, ride in a chariot and are followed by gift-bearing celebrants singing the wedding hymn.

The next morning the bride's parents would bring more gifts to the couple's home, giving their blessing to the union and encouraging their daughter to fulfill her primary goal as an Athenian wife: producing a male heir.

To the young bride, the customs of her wedding day must have seemed rather bewildering—and may even have left her feeling somewhat like a prisoner. In eating her husband's food, for instance, Demarete may have remembered the story of Persephone, who was forced against her will to stay with Hades, god of the underworld, after accepting from him just two pomegranate seeds. Indeed, the whole prenuptial ritual harked back to an earlier time, when the bride's change of abode was carried out as though it were a forcible abduction. Now, though only symbolic, the ritual was similar: First, the bride dons a veil and is seen as a stranger within her own home. Then she is carried off by the groom in a chariot, albeit a slow-moving one. And finally she is held captive in her new home.

Unlike the union of Persephone and Hades, however, this was not an unhappy affair. True, Demarete had not chosen Euphiletos; he had been her parents' choice. And she was doubtless more than a little awed by this great time of change. But she must have been excited about her new life, too, and the first years of her marriage were likely joyful ones. When she finally gave birth to a son, her happiness would have been complete.

Demarete's contentment must have been matched by that of her husband, especially after their son's birth. For a male heir was what every Athenian father desired, and the arrival of a son, whom we will call Mikion, fulfilled all of Euphiletos's expectations. As custom dictated, the proud father hung a wreath of olive leaves outside his front door to announce the good news to the world. Then he set about organizing the ceremony that formally welcomed the week-old baby boy into the household, and perhaps made plans to have Mikion registered in his phratry, a hereditary religious organization that scrutinized the legitimacy of children who would one day lay claim to an oikos.

Euphiletos must have considered himself to be the most blessed of men: He had a capable wife running his household—and one who was also "the chastest woman in all the

This mother reaching out to a baby in a highchair may have used a baby bottle like the one below, made of black glazed terra cotta and inscribed with the word *mamo*, or mommy.

city," in his opinion. As he was to tell the court that later heard his case, "She was a clever housewife, economical and exact in her management of everything." And now he had an heir who would one day inherit the family estate.

The young child responsible for all of this happiness would have spent his early years at home with Demarete. No doubt he played with the miniature wagons, rocking horses, hoops, and spinning tops that were popular with all Athenian children. And his mother and the servants who helped nurse Mikion must have passed the time by re-counting hair-raising tales of the bogeymen to which young Greeks loved to shiver: stories of Acco, who carried off bad children in her sack, or of Empusa, a hobgoblin who could change his shape at will, or of the terrifying Lamia, a princess robbed of her own children by the goddess Hera who took her revenge by eating the children of others. He would have heard, too, of the feats of Herakles, the tales of Achilles and Ajax and the other heroes of the Trojan War, and the story of Icarus flying too close to the sun.

As time passed, however, Demarete apparently began to feel less satisfied with her role. Except for Mikion's upbringing and the supervision of the household servants, she had little to occupy her time. Only for occasional visits to her own relatives or to the women in her neighborhood would she have ventured outside the four walls of Euphiletos's small, dark house, and there must have been times when she envied the servants, who at least got out of the house to go to the market for the daily shopping.

To Demarete this life of a respectable Athenian wife must have seemed far from the heady days when she first met Euphiletos. The immaturity of Athenian brides—and the wide age difference that was normal between husbands and wives—meant that they were unlikely to have any common friends. Moreover, husbands were away for much of the day, adhering to the Athenian saying that the sun should never catch them at home. For despite the importance of the household, the typ-ical Athenian male knew that his place was in the public arena—his role, to be out and about and attending to business. Most would have agreed with the sen-timents expressed by the historian Xenophon, "I certainly do not spend time indoors, for my wife is more than capable of managing everything inside the house." He continued, "For the woman it is more honorable to remain indoors than to be outside; for the man, it is more disgraceful."

Many Athenian wives were surely discontented by their isolation. Neglected by their spouses, some took to drink, some became scolds—and some found lovers.

In such circumstances, cooped up for long periods in the home, close daily contact

Two boys pull another one in a cart in this scene on a special type of pitcher used in an initiation rite. During the ceremony a boy would receive his first taste of wine, sym-bolizing the end of infancy.

between a mistress and her domestic servants—slaves—inevitably led to the development of strong bonds. And in Euphiletos's house there was one such slave to whom Demarete grew particularly close. Her name, too, goes unrecorded, but we will call her Melissa. During the many hours that Demarete had to spend confined in the women's quarters, the two had ample time to strike up an understanding and even a friendship. And the young bride had need of a friend at the beginning of her marriage, when she was still learning to do what society demanded of her. In time the trusted Melissa would come to perform yet another role for her restless mistress.

One of the few occasions when Athenian wives could respectably leave the home was to attend funerals. According to custom, the care of the deceased was very much a woman's task. On the day of death itself, the close female relatives would bathe the corpse, anoint it with oil, dress it, and lay it—covered with garlands—on a bier. A small coin was placed in the deceased's mouth as journey money, and beside the body was set a flask of oil and a honey cake as an offering to the gods of the underworld. Friends and neighbors would then come to pay their last respects, while women mourners, dressed in black and with their hair shorn, wailed lamentations. A vase of spring water would be set out in the street as a sign of the loss, and on leaving the house the visitors would wash their hands with the water as a symbolic gesture of purification.

Such rituals would have been performed when Demarete's mother-in-law died. A couple of days after her death, a solemn funeral procession set out from Euphiletos's house, and at its head was the corpse, covered by a cloak, carried on the bier. After Euphiletos, Demarete, and the other mourners reached the family tomb, the body was probably cremated, thus setting its spirit free, and the ashes buried in an urn. Then, after offerings were made and libations of wine and oil were poured on the grave,

the mourners would return to the house for a funeral banquet.

Among the eyes that fell on Demarete as she walked in the funeral cortege that day were those of a young Athenian man named Eratosthenes. It seems that he liked what he saw, and soon he was making inquiries about the identity of the attractive mourner and the house where she lived. This was not the first time that Eratosthenes had taken an interest in another man's wife. Perhaps, like Casanova in a later age, he needed a bit of danger to add spice to his sexual adventures and found that the pursuit of a wife under the nose of an unsuspecting husband offered greater thrills. In any case, he set his sights on Demarete and devised an elaborate plan for winning her affections.

Eratosthenes' first problem lay in making contact—no easy achievement when Demarete spent her days shut away behind locked doors. But soon he found a way via Melissa. Watching Euphiletos's house, he quickly discovered that the slave woman left each day to go to the market. One morning he approached her and secured her agreement to take a message to her mistress.

The effect on Demarete of that first communication must have been dramatic. Young and probably bored to distraction, she was evidently open to advances, and under the pretext of attending a women's religious festival, she decided to meet with Eratosthenes. Then, throwing caution to the wind, she agreed to receive her lover secretly at her own home, taking advantage of a recent change in her living arrangements with Euphiletos.

Like most Athenian dwellings, Euphiletos's house occupied two floors, the upper rooms being reserved for the women and the more public lower rooms for the men. But the demands of parenting had revealed a defect in this layout: The baby had to be bathed on the ground floor, where water could be fetched easily, and the stairs connecting the two stories were dangerous for a young mother to negotiate with an infant in her arms. Accordingly, Euphiletos had suggested that the normal order of things be reversed, that he move upstairs while Demarete and the

THE HEALING ARTS

Hippocrates is renowned for the oath named for him and is shown here with the caduceus, a healing snake coiled about a staff that would become a symbol of the medical profession. Information about him is scarce, however, and he may not be the author of the texts that bear his name.

In Greek mythology, sickness and disease afflicted the human race when Pandora, the first woman, released these troubles from a large jar. According to the myth, only hope remained to console mankind. But Greeks of the fifth and fourth centuries BC decided hope was not enough; they began to observe and investigate the causes of diseases in an attempt to discover ways to alleviate or even cure them.

Among the physicians of the ancient world, none is more famous than Hippocrates, who is thought to have headed a medical school on the island of Kos in the eastern Aegean. Although it is now believed that most of the so-called Hippocratic writings were authored by his students or by later physicians, these treatises—which consider such subjects as pathology, physiology, embryology, gynecology, and surgery—mark the beginnings of systematic medical inquiry in Greece.

Hippocrates and his colleagues believed that illness was caused either by an imbalance of bodily fluids or by external

Scalpel in hand, a physician lets blood from a patient. Other treatments included herbs, plasters, and dressings.

43

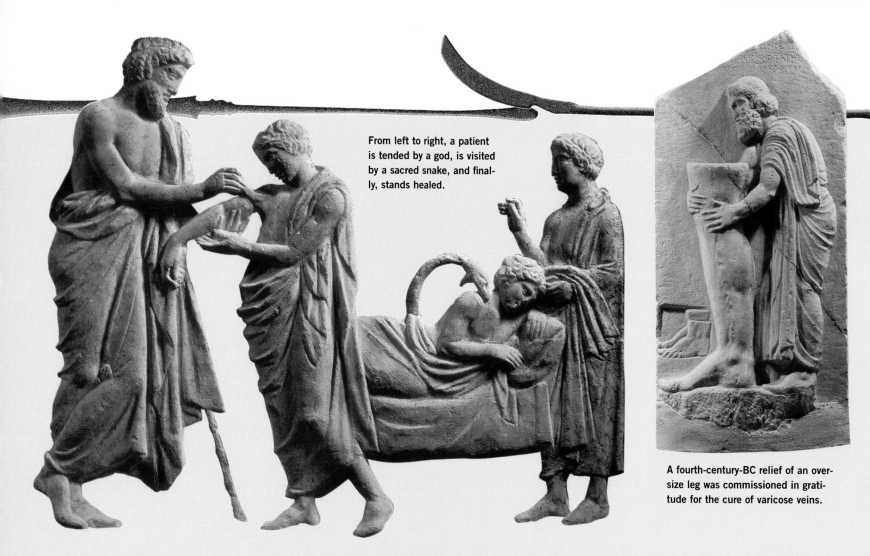

From left to right, a patient is tended by a god, is visited by a sacred snake, and finally, stands healed.

A fourth-century-BC relief of an oversize leg was commissioned in gratitude for the cure of varicose veins.

factors like sun, air, and climate. After examining the patient, a doctor might prescribe a variety of treatments to restore bodily harmony, among them proper diet, exercise, baths, drugs, bloodletting, purges, and surgery.

In ancient Greece, however, doctors had no monopoly on the treatment of illness. Therapeutic care was provided by herbalists, midwives, drug sellers, and gymnasium trainers. The Greeks also did not forget the importance of the gods in charting the course of human lives, and so turned to charms and incantations as a way of asking the deities for help, especially in the case of chronic or life-threatening diseases. To aid those seeking divine healing, a special cult surrounding the god Asklepios arose simultaneously with the development of Hippocratic medicine.

As the patron of both patients and doctors, Asklepios was the deity most associated with healing. Ailing pilgrims would make their way to the god's principal temple at Epidaurus, about 50 miles southwest of Athens. There they would be purified in a bathing pavilion, therapeutically massaged by a priest-doctor, dressed in white robes and olive wreaths, and laid on a bed for incubation—a ritual, dream-filled sleep in which the god or his sacred snake would bring a cure.

Faith healing, or temple medicine, probably coexisted peaceably with Hippocratic medicine. Indeed, for serious illness, physicians might actually entrust patients to the higher powers of Asklepios, a god whose name is even invoked in the vow taken by new doctors—the Hippocratic oath.

THE HIPPOCRATIC OATH

I swear by Apollo Physician and Asklepios and Hygieia and Panacea and all the gods and goddesses, making them my witnesses, that I will fulfill according to my ability and judgment this oath and this covenant. . . .

I will use my regimen for the benefit of the sick according to my ability and judgment; I will keep them from harm and injustice.

I will neither give a deadly drug to anybody if asked for it, nor will I make a suggestion to this effect. Similarly I will not give to a woman an abortive remedy. In purity and holiness I will guard my life and my art.

I will not use the knife, not even on sufferers from stone, but will withdraw in favor of such men as are engaged in this work.

Whatever houses I may visit, I will come for the benefit of the sick, remaining free of all intentional injustice, of all mischief and in particular of sexual relations with both women and men, be they free or slaves.

What I may see or hear in the course of the treatment or even outside of the treatment in regard to the life of men, which on no account one must spread abroad, I will keep to myself concealing such things as if they were religious secrets.

If I fulfill this oath and do not violate it, may it be granted to me to enjoy life and art, being honored with fame among all men for all time to come; if I transgress it and swear falsely, may the opposite of all this be my lot.

baby install themselves in the lower rooms giving onto the street.

Despite the risk of creating trouble for himself by increasing his wife's exposure to the outside world, then, Euphiletos had taken over the upper floor. And it was this rearrangement of the home that now came to Eratosthenes' aid: He was able to slip unseen into Demarete's ground-floor room with an ease that would never have been possible if the women's quarters had remained upstairs.

Even so, the young lovers had some narrow escapes. Once Euphiletos came back unexpectedly from the countryside when Eratosthenes was due for a visit. Rather than cancel the tryst, however, Demarete enlisted Melissa's help to hoodwink Euphiletos. That evening, husband and wife dined together upstairs as usual, but just as they finished eating they were disturbed by the sound of Mikion crying. Euphiletos told Demarete to go and feed him—not knowing that, at Demarete's suggestion, Melissa had been deliberately pinching the baby to make him squeal.

At first Demarete feigned unwillingness to leave her husband. When Euphiletos insisted, she eventually agreed to go downstairs, but only after teasing him that he wanted to get rid of her so he could flirt with the house's serving maid. "You mauled her about before when you were drunk!" Demarete told him in mock accusation. Then she bade him good-night, left the room, and locked the door behind her.

Apparently, Euphiletos gave little thought to the locked door. During the night, however, he was awakened by an unexpected noise, the sound of the front door creaking. Toward morning, when his wife came back upstairs, he asked her about the noise. The baby's bedside lamp had gone out, Demarete explained, and she had slipped across to a neighbor's house to relight it. Euphiletos seemed happy enough with the explanation, though he could not help noticing something else—traces of powder and rouge on Demarete's face, surely an unusual thing at that early hour of the day.

Despite the close call, Euphiletos seems to have thought no more about the incident, and Demarete was able to continue her dangerous liaison undisturbed, taking full advantage of her husband's frequent trips to the countryside by planning further meetings with her lover. The arrangement might have gone on indefinitely, in fact, if news of the affair had not reached the ears of one of Eratosthenes' former mistresses. Consumed by jealousy and determined to get back at her one-time lover, the woman decided to let Euphiletos know what was going on behind his back.

Even in the grip of anger, the abandoned mistress knew that she could not approach a man that she did not know in the street. So she gave the job to an old woman of her acquaintance, taking advantage of the somewhat greater freedom that those past childbearing age had to move around the city. This aged envoy waited for Euphiletos near his house, then waylaid him with her terrible message.

Euphiletos listened in amazement and horror. He learned that his wife had been unfaithful to him in his own house over a period of weeks, perhaps months. He was told exactly who it was that had been cuckolding him. And he discovered that Demarete was not the only married woman that Eratosthenes had seduced. "There are plenty of others," the old woman assured him. "It's his profession!"

Cropped hair and tattooed arms and neck identify this young Thracian woman as a slave.

Suddenly small incidents like the creaking door began to flood back into Euphiletos's head. Now he wanted one thing above all else, to find out the whole truth. And there was only one person who could tell him, other than his wife and her lover—Demarete's confidante, Melissa.

Returning home at once, Euphiletos told the slave that he wanted her to go with him to do some shopping. Instead of heading to the market, however, Euphiletos took her to a friend's house, where he could interrogate her without fear of interruption. There he told her that he had discovered what had been going on in his house. Melissa pleaded ignorance, but Euphiletos would have none of it: Unless she told him the whole truth, he would have her flogged and sent to work in the mills.

This was a fearsome threat, for being condemned to the back-breaking labor involved in grinding flour was a fate that every Athenian slave dreaded. The Roman novelist Apuleius would describe such institutions over half a millennium later, and little had changed in the intervening years. "The men there were indescribable," he wrote. "Their entire skin was colored black and blue with the weals left by whippings." He continued, "They were sallow and discolored, and the smoky and steamy atmosphere had affected their eyelids and inflamed their eyes."

The prospect of exchanging the relatively easy life of a lady's maid for that kind of existence must have been terrifying for Melissa. Still, she continued to hold out, denying any knowledge of the accusations. Only when Euphiletos told her that he even knew Eratosthenes' name did she finally give in. After extracting a promise from Euphiletos that he would not punish her for her role in the affair, she told him everything she knew. But her master wanted more. "I expect

A child slave fastens her mistress's shoe. Most slaves were captives, but poor foreigners were said to sell their own children.

you to show me this actually happening," he said. The next time Eratosthenes came to the house, he told her, Melissa was to inform him. The betrayed husband wanted to catch his wife and her lover in the act.

Euphiletos did not have long to wait. It was less than a week later, on his way back from the country, that he met a friend and invited him home for dinner. As was customary in such circumstances, the men ate alone, served by slaves. When the meal was over, the visitor departed for his own house and Euphiletos settled down to sleep. The next thing he knew was that Melissa had entered his room and was whispering in his ear: Eratosthenes was in the house.

Euphiletos already knew exactly what he had to do. He needed witnesses for the scene that was about to unfold; hence his nocturnal circuit of the neighborhood in search of fellow citizens whose word would be good in a court of law. And when he had gathered a sufficient number, he set off back toward his home.

Along the way he stopped at the home of a torch-maker to buy some torches: The band of witnesses would need light so there could be no mistaking what they were about to see.

Arriving at the house, Euphiletos gestured to the others to be quiet. Silently, he led the group through the front door, which Melissa had left unbarred, as instructed. Then he made straight for his wife's room. Forcing open the door, he burst in—and there, in the torches' flickering light, many eyes saw just what he had expected and feared: a flash of bare flesh as the lovers struggled to cover their nakedness, the look of animal fear as they realized that there was no escape.

Euphiletos strode across the room and knocked Eratosthenes to the ground. Grabbing a piece of rope, he then tied the naked man's hands behind his back. Pathetically, Eratosthenes begged for his life, offering to pay Euphiletos compensation for the wrong he had done him. But Euphiletos was in no mood to listen. He brandished a weapon, probably a knife, indicating that he had made up his mind what he was going to do to the intruder. "It is not I who shall be killing you," he declared, full of the righteous anger of a true Athenian, "but the law of the state, which you, in transgressing, have valued less highly than your own pleasure." Then, in the words that Euphiletos used at his subsequent trial, Eratosthenes "met the fate which the laws prescribe for wrongdoers of his kind."

In casting himself as the instrument of justice, Euphiletos would represent the killing of Eratosthenes as his duty as well as his right. And, indeed, Athenian law was clear on the subject: To protect the integrity of the oikos, a householder could kill an adulterer taken red-handed in his own home. The law in Athens was by no means the harshest on the subject of adultery, however: On the island of Tenedos in the eastern Aegean, for example, the injured husband was allowed to kill both partners with an ax.

In the Athenian justice system, the crime of rape posed less of a threat to the household than adultery, and its penalty was merely a monetary fine. The reasoning behind this was that while only the wife suffered at the hands of a rapist, an adulterer jeopardized the stability of the entire family by stealing a wife's affection for her husband. As Euphiletos would argue at his trial, "He who achieves his ends by persuasion thereby corrupts the mind as well as the body of the woman." In addition, Euphiletos continued, such a man "gains access to all a man's possessions, and casts doubts on his children's parentage."

This last point was of crucial importance. For the law was determined to preserve legitimate inheritance within the oikos in order to control the composition of the state. Rape involved a single known act of copulation, and any resultant issue could be dealt with by abortion or exposure (this last was achieved by abandoning children in temples where they could be adopted by strangers—or on hillsides where they would die). But adultery im-

At the sanctuary of Artemis at Brauron in eastern Attica, young Athenian girls participated in a rite of passage that marked their transition from childhood to womanhood. Part of the ritual required them to perform a dance that imitated the movements of a bear, perhaps symbolizing the girls' last opportunity to behave with abandon before taking on the responsibilities of adult life. A statue and bas-relief from the sanctuary (below) show worshipers with animals probably destined to be sacrificed to the goddess.

plied an ongoing sexual relationship, creating the risk that any children born to the wife at any time might be illegitimate. It was this consideration that made adultery a public as well as a private offense.

Euphiletos's right to take Eratosthenes' life, then, was apparently not in question. And when the case eventually came to trial, Euphiletos was not charged simply with being responsible for the young man's death, which he never sought to deny. Rather, he was accused by members of Eratosthenes' family of having deliberately set out to entrap the lovers, thereby turning a case of self-defense—defense of the household—into one of premeditated murder; and this *was* a capital offense. They also claimed that the victim had been killed not in the bedroom but at the hearth, a part of the house that was sacred to the goddess Hestia; killing a man there was considered a sacrilegious act. And they implied, too, that Euphiletos may have had other reasons for wanting Eratosthenes dead besides the obvious motive of injured pride.

In his defense, Euphiletos took pains to deny all of these charges. First, he provided circumstantial arguments to show that he had not planned the murder, citing the fact that he had innocently invited a friend back to his house for dinner that evening.

Second, he was able to call on his witnesses to refute any suggestion that the victim had died anywhere but the bedroom. And third, he pointed to the fact that he had never set eyes on Eratosthenes before the night of the killing as proof that he had had no secondary motive for wishing him dead. Although he could have done so, Euphiletos seems not to have offered evidence in court from Melissa. Since slaves' testimony was extracted by torture, they were prone to say whatever they thought their interrogators wanted to hear. There was, therefore, a feeling that slave evidence was not particularly reliable.

All of this is evident from the surviving documents. But then the record goes blank. Through one of history's cruel silences, we do not know the verdict of the jurors assembled to hear the case. In all probability,

back in Athens's slave market, assuming, of course, that Euphiletos kept his promise and did not send her to the mills.

Such speculation seems reasonable. What is less clear, however, are Euphiletos's motives. All that we know about the lives of this family from fifth-century-BC Athens comes from the carefully crafted account that he delivered at the time of his trial. And although he depicts himself as a trusting, almost comic figure—though one capable of deadly violence—we may wonder whether he really was as gullible as he would have us believe. He allows Demarete to lock him in his room without voicing any suspicion. The front door creaks in the night but he readily accepts his wife's explanation. He notices the makeup on her face and says nothing.

We will never know for sure just how in-

"He who achieves his ends by persuasion thereby corrupts the mind as well as the body of the woman."

however, it is likely that Euphiletos went free. He had prepared his defense well, and the jurors who passed judgment on him would have needed little convincing of the enormity of Eratosthenes' crime, threatening as it did the family and, by extension, society itself.

As for the fate of the other characters in the drama, we can only guess. Demarete would have been publicly dishonored by the exposure of her infidelity and would have been banned from visiting any of the city's temples or attending its religious festivals. Undoubtedly, Euphiletos would have divorced her, as he was, in fact, legally required to do unless he wanted to lose his own citizenship rights; Demarete was probably sent back to her family in disgrace. In all likelihood Euphiletos also decided to dispense with Melissa's services, and she would have found herself

nocent Euphiletos was in this whole affair. Unlike the great figures who strode the Athenian stage during the city's golden age—Pericles, for example, or Aspasia, both of whom we shall meet in the next chapter—Euphiletos and Demarete disappear from the public eye after the court case.

And so the players in this drama faded back into the obscurity from which they came. Then, as now, sensationalism made news of the happenings in an otherwise unexceptional Greek household and perpetuated the memory of a husband's bitter moment of awakening and the violent response that it provoked on one hot Athenian night. Once the issue was finally settled one way or the other, people's interests turned elsewhere, to fresh scandals and dramas played out in the lives of the powerful and the rich.

WINNING GLORY AT THE GAMES

Every four years, Greek statesmen and peasants, merchants and philosophers traveled the roads and waterways leading to Olympia, a sacred place situated in a grassy plain on the bank of the Alpheios River. Most people camped wherever they could find space, although important visitors found accommodations in the site's magnificent guesthouse. A festival atmosphere prevailed as hawkers peddled their wares, old friends reunited, orators expounded their ideas, and men consumed vast quantities of food and drink. It was noisy, hot, and crowded. Nevertheless, thousands returned time and time again because Olympia offered something unique: the best athletes in the Greek world fighting for supremacy in its most prestigious contest—the Olympic Games.

Olympia's contest was part of a quartet of important Panhellenic athletic events known as the crown games for the wreaths awarded to the winners *(above)*. The games' origins were intertwined with Greek mythology. Herakles, for instance, is credited with founding the sanctuary of Olympia and instituting the games centuries before the first recorded Olympic Games in 776 BC. It is more likely, however, that purely mortal beings originally established the site for funeral games honoring local heroes.

Like Olympia's event, the Pythian Games, in Delphi, took place every four years, while the Isthmian Games, near Corinth, and the Nemean Games, in the Argolid, ran biennially. To enable athletes to compete in all four contests, officials staggered the scheduling by years. Any free Greek male in good standing could enter, including

Victor with wreath crowns

those living abroad in the colonies as well as those living in the nearby city-states. Associated costs limited the number of less affluent participants, however, since an athlete might have to pay a professional trainer, purchase equipment, pay for travel, and leave his job to compete. In order to enter the Olympic Games, athletes were asked to swear that they had been in training for 10 months and then train for an additional 30 days in Olympia. Women, barred from entering—or even viewing—the crown games, held their own contest at Olympia. Consisting of just three footraces, the Heraia, as the event was called, honored the goddess Hera.

Like the Heraia, the crown games each paid homage to a chosen deity, and temples, altars, sacred groves, and monuments to the gods dotted all four locations. Within the confines of these sacred places, officials made animal sacrifices, athletes and judges swore their game oaths, supplicants consulted the oracles, and winners paraded. Of course, the sites also encompassed impressive athletic facilities. Chariots raced around the hippodrome, the largest outdoor racecourse, while runners flew down the stretch of the stadium. The gymnasium's open courtyard provided additional running tracks and areas for discus and javelin throwing, and its covered area could be used for practice during bad weather. In the *palaistra*, also partially enclosed as a rule, jumpers, boxers, and wrestlers trained for their competitions. Some of the facility's back rooms were set aside for bathing and socializing.

Throughout the Greek world, athletes represented an ideal of human accomplishment, and truces were declared in times of war so that all eligible Greeks could participate in the games without fear. The competitions, generally performed in the nude, celebrated the godlike qualities inherent in man. Victory brought great fame and glory both to the athletes and to their families and hometown. A fifth-century-BC Olympic winner named Diagoras fathered two sons who in turn won Olympic crowns at the 448 BC games. The devoted sons placed their wreaths on Diagoras's head and carried him about the stadium on their shoulders. A friend called out as they passed, saying in essence: Die now, Diagoras, for you have nothing but the heights of Olympus left to scale.

This marble statue, when complete, portrayed a victor tying a ribbon of victory, or fillet, around his head. A garland of greenery was placed over the band on the final day of the games, when all of the winners paraded proudly past the altar of their games' patron god. Although his material prize at the games might have been a simple wreath, once he returned home, a winner often was honored with statues of himself and specially composed songs as well as cash bonuses, free meals from the state, and various other lifelong privileges.

An attendant massages the back of a competitor, whose trainer *(right)* gives him some advice on the finer points of his sport.

One athlete helps another clean up with water *(above)* as a third *(right)* scrapes off oil and dirt with a strigil *(below)*.

Horses running full out, a chariot driver *(left)* races at the hippodrome, competing in one of the most popular, as well as most dangerous, contests of the games. Great skill and confidence–captured in the self-assured countenance of the Charioteer of Delphi at right–was demanded when rounding the turning posts at either end of the arena, where too often wheels would lock, horses collide, and chariots overturn. While the drivers risked crippling injury and death, the owners of the rigs reaped the glory of a win.

55

Body twisting and arm swinging back, a *discobolos* prepares to hurl a discus like the inscribed bronze one at left.

The pentathlon, a contest for best all-around athlete, consisted of five events: running, wrestling, discus throwing, javelin throwing, and jumping. In the scene above, a jumper swings his arms forward using weights to increase his distance while his trainer and another competitor watch. At right, two wrestlers engage in a combination event called the *pankration,* overseen by a judge prepared to strike if they get too rough. Nearby, two boxers punch it out.

Youthful runners sprint toward the finish line in a footrace, the most popular of all the sports. The racing distance varied from one stadium length to as many as 24. A special type of race featured armored participants weighted down with shield, helmet, and greaves.

CHAPTER TWO

THE SCHOOL OF GREECE

Builder, democrat, statesman, and general, Pericles was the guiding spirit of Athens's golden age. Even though he was an aristocrat, Pericles took pride in Athenians of all classes. "In my opinion," he declared, "each single one of our citizens is able to show himself the rightful lord and owner of his own person, and to do this moreover, with exceptional grace and versatility."

Another eight years would pass before he voiced his thoughts in words that the historian Thucydides would immortalize as the Funeral Oration. But even now, as he stepped along the Panathenaic Way en route to the Acropolis, the folds of his woolen tunic rippling with every stride, the Athenian statesman Pericles could have looked in any direction and heard in his mind a few of the words he would deliver years later: "Our city is the school of Greece." Come to this place, he could have told any of those around him, and you come to learn—to sit at the feet of its gifted teachers and philosophers, to gaze upon the works of the Athenian empire's most celebrated artists and artisans, to see in action a democracy that "favors the many and not the few."

All around him, as he made his way through the almost fluid sunshine of this Mediterranean morning in 438 BC, his city spoke of greatness. The huge paving stones beneath his sandaled feet were nothing less than the building blocks of an empire that encompassed much of the Aegean, while the high wall that enclosed the city made Athens an enclave all but impervious to its enemies. Rare indeed, a confident Pericles must often have thought, was the enemy foolhardy enough to attempt a siege of such defenses.

This silver Athenian coin carries on one side the profile of Athena, patron goddess of the city, and on the other side her emblems—the owl and the olive branch. Coins like this one circulated throughout the Aegean in the time of Pericles.

Like nearly everyone else in Athens, Pericles had been up this morning with the sun and had probably dined on the typical breakfast of bread soaked in wine, perhaps chased down by a few olives or figs. Yet unlike most men, who hurried off without a thought for their wives, he had left his home as he left it every morning, by sharing a long kiss with the woman in his life, the beautiful Aspasia.

But now, striding out along the Panathenaic Way, the city's main northwest-to-southeast thoroughfare, Pericles' thoughts were on the business of the day—and on the sights and sounds that surrounded him. Ahead he could see two of the city's newer buildings. Crowning a hill off to his right was a temple under construction, its forest of columns rising toward a roof that was still far from complete. This was the Temple of Hephaistos, named after the god of fire and artisans, a deity held in high esteem by a city that took such pride in workmanship. And farther on up the road, on the left-hand side, stood the Stoa Poikile, or Painted Portico. Constructed of limestone and marble, the building was a kind of museum, the place, according to one Greek orator, where "the memorials of all our noble deeds are depicted." Enshrined inside, as every Athenian schoolboy knew, were murals that celebrated victories against the Trojans and the Persians, and other high points of the city's historical and mythological heritage.

Already, though, Pericles could sense the energy, the buzz of commerce, that lay ahead. He could see the mottled plane trees, tall cypresses, and leafy elms that sheltered the city's marketplace and, shifting ceaselessly beneath them, the throngs of shoppers and merchants who made every midmorning the market rush hour. Passing the Stoa Poikile, he entered the Agora.

The Agora was the very heart of fifth-century-BC Athens, its commercial and civic hub. It was here, framing the spacious open marketplace, that the city fathers had also located the administrative buildings of the state. Looking to his right, above the heads of the shoppers and beyond the boundary stones that marked the limits of the Agora, Pericles saw a row of imposing public buildings. There stood the bouleuterion, where the boule, Athens's 500-member administrative council, sat in session, each member wearing a wreath of myrtle as a badge of honor. Next to the council building Pericles could see the distinctive shape of the tholos, the circular building where council members passed the night, ready to respond to any emergency. And beside the tholos was the *strategeion,* the generals' headquarters.

Pericles would have been all too familiar with this last structure. Although he was in his midfifties, Pericles still occupied the office of *strategos* that he had held since his early forties. A strategos was a general, 10 of whom were elected annually to form the high command of the state's armed forces and who together were among the most powerful individuals in the democracy. As a strategos, Pericles occupied one of the few offices in Athens that allowed for reelection. Most other officials served a single term and were sometimes barred for life from ever again holding the same position.

Still, Pericles and the other *strategoi* did have to answer to the *ekklesia,* the assembly of the people. Raising his eyes toward the southwest, he would have seen the assembly's open-air venue on a nearby hill known as the Pnyx. Had the assembly been meeting that day, all citizens over 18 would have been entitled, if not expected, to participate in that body's deliberations. On occasion lingerers in the Agora were even rounded up and forcibly funneled in the direction of the Pnyx by policemen wielding a rope dripping wet with vermilion dye. Theoretically at least, anyone who managed to slip under the rope would have his dereliction of duty splashed all over his tunic.

For his part, Pericles could hardly have respected such shirkers, siding as he did with those Athenians who "regard a man who takes no interest in public affairs not as apathetic, but as completely useless."

Pericles' own preeminence was founded partly on his skill in

A 19th-century drawing depicts the Agora as it was—the very heart of Athens, the center of its civic activity, and its commercial hub.

Under the watchful eye of Athena *(center)*, legendary Greek warriors cast their votes with pebbles in this representation of democracy in action.

THE DEMOCRATIC PROCESS

By the middle of the fifth century BC, Athens had developed the most advanced political system in the Greek world, one in which the *demos*–the people–ruled supreme. The Athenians called this system *demokratia;* we know it as democracy.

Central to the Athenian democratic system was the *ekklesia,* or assembly of the people, the city-state's main deliberative and decision-making institution. All citizens, or freeborn Athenian men, could attend the assembly; out of 50,000 eligible citizens, some 6,000 regularly did.

The ekklesia made decisions that were binding on the whole community, but only after the issue under consideration was duly debated. Any citizen could participate in the discourse by standing up and trying to persuade the assembly on a course of action. Voting en masse on each issue before them, citizens would indicate their decisions by raising their hands. All votes were equal, and the majority ruled. A smaller council of 500 citizens, called the boule, prepared the agenda for the assembly and was responsible for day-to-day administration of the state's affairs.

The hollow post on the bronze jury ballot above indicated a vote for conviction—the solid post at right, acquittal.

To vote for ostracism, Athenian citizens scratched the offender's name on a piece of pottery known as an *ostrakon (right)*.

Athenian law courts completed the task of carrying out the mandates of the people. Accessible to all citizens, the courts were charged with interpreting and applying the laws of Athens. Court rulings were made by juries that numbered anywhere from 201 to 2,500, their large size considered a means of avoiding corruption.

Juries, as well as council members and most of the city's executive officers, were selected by lot from the entire citizen body as a way of preventing any single man from becoming too powerful. But should this safeguard fail, Athenian democracy had another—somewhat more drastic—method of dealing with aspiring dictators. If 6,000 citizens cast their votes against him in the assembly, the offending citizen faced ostracism—banishment from the city for 10 years.

Water clocks kept proceedings moving in court: Water flowing from the higher pot to the lower measured the time left to a speaker. This pot held about six minutes' worth of water.

speaking to those who gathered at the Pnyx—his effect as galvanic as "a dread thunderbolt," said one observer. Indeed, as an orator and proposer of laws, he so dominated the assembly that Thucydides claimed that Athens was "in name a democracy, but in fact a government by the greatest citizen." However, it was through the democracy that Pericles exercised this authority.

The fundamental institutions of that democracy had been put in place toward the end of the sixth century BC, when power had for the first time passed into the hands of ordinary citizens, regardless of their wealth or class. Thereafter, members of the lower classes could rise to the highest positions in the Athenian government. Pericles had promoted other kinds of constitutional changes as well, ending the longstanding practice of granting citizenship to the children of Athenian fathers and foreign-born mothers, for example. The general also introduced jury pay, a popular measure that made it easier for poorer citizens to serve on juries without having to worry about the time lost from work.

This last measure had helped to give Pericles a secure base of support, but he would later have cause to regret the change in the citizenship law. His first wife, Athenian by birth, had given him two sons, both of whom were entitled to citizenship under the new law. But both were destined to die in a plague that swept through Athens beginning in 430 BC. This left Pericles with only one heir—a third son, Pericles the younger. This son had been born to Aspasia, however, who was not only the general's common-law wife but also one of Athens's many metics, the city's population of resident foreigners. Under the terms of the new law, their son could not be a citizen, and Pericles found himself in the prickly position of having to petition the assembly for an exemption from his own law in order to legitimize his namesake.

Such thoughts were not on Pericles' mind as he strode purposefully through the Agora that morning. Here he was in his own element, surrounded mostly by men, many of them citizens like himself, the rest mostly metics and slaves. Proper women stayed home, chastely ensconced in their own quarters in their own houses; only slaves, poor women forced by circumstances to make a living outside the home, or female metics—themselves unhindered by the usual restrictions imposed on the wives and daughters of citizens—could mingle freely with men in the city.

Moving through the Agora of cosmopolitan Athens, Pericles would have been able to distinguish the different types of people around him with little difficulty. For example, he would have picked out the visiting foreigners by their hats—Athenians rarely wore headgear, even in the noonday sun—and members of the lowest orders by their lack of footwear. Time and again he would have paused to acknowledge the greetings of city officials, raising his hand in salutation in the Greek manner. For the most part, though, he would have walked as just another citizen, his gait unslowed by others, either the merely curious or the patently intrusive. In democratic Athens, where everyone was expected to walk, none would have thought it unusual that the man who was king in all but title should be out and about and on foot.

In cutting across the marketplace, Pericles may well have nodded to some of the soldiers' widows who generally sold ribbons and wreaths, or heard female slaves hawking shoes or secondhand clothing. Those few things, however, only scratched the surface of what shoppers could find in the Agora. Early that morning, long before Pericles said goodbye to Aspasia with their customary kiss, peasants from the Attic countryside surrounding Athens had made their way along the alleys that led toward the Agora, some dressed in the skins and leggings common to drovers and urging sheep or goats to market with switches. Others, farmers from beyond the city's walls, had ferried produce and firewood into town, their carts creaking on solid wheels along dirt streets lined with shops and workshops.

Food and clothing of all kinds could be bought at the market, as could books, pottery, and hardware. The buying and sell-ing of slaves was another important trade in the Agora. So heavy was the traffic in human beings in the fifth century BC, in fact, that the duty on imported slaves was a significant source of the Athenian government's revenue.

Shopkeepers laid out their wares on tables set inside wicker booths topped by awnings, giving the Agora the air of an on-going carnival. There was, however, method to the apparent madness of this open-air bazaar. Merchants, many of whom paid a fee to set up shop in the market, were grouped according to the products they sold; hence, all the sandalmakers would be in one area, all the wine dealers in another, and so on. Over time their customers had grown so used to this arrangement that they spoke of going "to the pots" to buy pottery or "to the slaves" to make a deal for a new servant.

It was easy to locate the area where food could be bought in the marketplace. The aromas of fish, strong cheese, olives swimming in brine, fruity new wines, freshly picked apples and pome-granates, and vegetables of all kinds swam in the air and mingled

Olives and the oil pressed from them, shown at left being sold in jars, were a staple of the Greek economy.

with the more robust fragrances of oxen, donkeys, sheep, and pigs. At the same time, the aroma of cooked food also percolated in the steamy air, made steamier still as the sun rose higher in the sky.

Noise, too, was inescapable in the Agora. Clowns, dancers, jugglers, conjurers, and entertainers of every description performed. Shopkeepers exhorted passersby to check out their goods or to come in for a taste of herbed porridge, heady with mint or thyme. And people shouted to one another, argued with thieving merchants, or cursed the particularly rapacious to Hades and back.

Adding to the bedlam were the many peddlers who carried their wares on tables slung from shoulder straps and who strolled the area, calling out to attract customers. Porters, too, noisily worked the crowd, offering to lug purchases to shoppers' homes, while from the porticoes

men frequently did the shopping, scurry off to buy groceries.

And it was here, in the market, that Pericles would often have picked out the familiar form of a well-known Athenian, the disheveled and barefoot Socrates. Because of his broad nose, large, fleshy mouth, and protruding eyes, even his friends compared the philosopher to a satyr, one of the animal-like attendants of Dionysos, god of wine and fertility. Shuffling along the Panathenaic Way with his characteristic waddling gait, asking questions, forcing those around him to recognize how little they understood of the tenets by which they lived, Socrates was regularly accompanied by a gaggle of students.

By now, though, Pericles was nearing the far side of the Agora. There he might well have paused to drink at the fountain house next to the city's

"A general must not only have clean hands, Sophocles, but clean eyes, as well."

of the various public buildings on the perimeter of the marketplace, a drone of voices formed a low counterpoint to the cacophony of the market itself. Only those who practiced the particularly unsavory habit of carrying their loose change in their mouths were silent for any length of time, and then not for long.

Not everyone went to the Agora to shop or to sell, of course. Some, like Pericles, were only passing through en route to other parts of the city. Many more spent the morning, *every* morning in fact, idling in the market, and the center of the Agora was purposely left free of booths in order to accommodate this group. It was here that men could catch up on the latest gossip or spread some of their own, debate the hot political issues of the moment, or second-guess the most recent court verdicts. Some of them would slip away from time to time to tend to business or, since

red-roofed mint before turning his back on the hubbub of the marketplace. For all his interest in the common good, he was by no means a man of the people, and he had no desire to spend any more time rubbing elbows with ordinary citizens than he had to. Aloof to the point of arrogance, he preferred the company of a few close friends or, better yet, his own company. As a result, he rarely socialized and took pains to avoid public appearances, courting the masses only in his walks, such as today's outing, and then only along the one street that linked those most public of places, the Agora and the Acropolis.

Experience had shown him to be prudent in keeping to himself. The writer Plutarch would later recount how Pericles was once accosted in the Agora by a heckler who followed him around all day heaping abuse at every turn. The general, displaying remarkable self-control, bit his tongue and did his best to ignore his tormentor. But the man would not be put off and instead followed Pericles right to his own doorstep, spewing obscenities all the while. Pericles, unflappable to the end, stoically bore it all. Mindful only of the increasing darkness, the general quietly ordered a servant "to take a torch," as Plutarch later reported, "and escort the fellow in safety back to his own home."

For his failure to fight back, Pericles drew only renewed scorn from his detractors, many of whom read the great man's reserve as conceit. To his friends, however, Pericles was anything but conceited, even if his idea of a good time was the kind of philosophical discussion that left the average person numb. Still, he was not averse to putting his friends in their place—and with a touch of humor at that. Such was the case in 441 BC when Pericles and the playwright Sophocles were both serving as generals. The two men were leading the fleet in an expedition against a hostile island in the eastern Aegean, when Sophocles, who had an eye for young men as well as women, cast an approving glance at a particularly comely youth. Pericles wasted no time in reminding his friend of his position: "A general must not only have clean hands, Sophocles, but clean eyes, as well."

Whatever else people thought of him, Pericles knew in his own heart that his intentions had always been pure and had been motivated solely by love for Athens. So what if he was aloof; it was not in his nature to be the friend of every man, but rather the leader of all. And as for arrogance, Pericles might have told his enemies to look at the past and see what arrogance had wrought.

Without question, much of what Pericles had passed in the course of his walk had been erected in his own lifetime, "a time of many changes," as he would later portray it, and had often been erected at his urging. But Pericles, stepping off the last quarter mile of the Panathenaic Way and peering up at the looming

THE POTTER'S ART

Athenian potters, portrayed practicing their craft on the vase below, produced ceramic ware that was acclaimed around the Mediterranean. A pot's function determined its shape; shown at right are some of the types. At the top is a kylix, or drinking cup; in the second row are two storage jars, a pelike and an amphora, and a lekythos for holding funerary oil; in the bottom row are a widemouthed krater for mixing water and wine, an alabastron for perfume, and a loutrophoros, a water jar for a bride's ritual bath.

Acropolis, was pegging his hopes for what the Greeks called *kleos aphthiton*—the fame and glory that outlasted death—on an even grander statement in stone. Above him, now nearing completion on Athens's sacred mount, was a temple that would forever be associated with the city's golden age and with Pericles himself: the Parthenon.

The Acropolis had long been the location of temples and shrines, among them an older version of the Parthenon. But they had been destroyed by invading Persians 40 years earlier and had for the most part been left in ruins by the Athenians as a monument to Persian aggression. More urgent in the aftermath of the Persian withdrawal was the need to rebuild the city's demolished walls, after which the people of Athens turned their attention to the reconstruction of both the Agora and their own ruined homes.

While all this was going on in the 470s, the teenaged Pericles and his parents were experiencing one of the pendulum swings that sometimes characterized Athenian democracy. Only a few years earlier, in 484 BC, his father, a military and political leader named Xanthippos, had been ostracized by a vote of the assembly and, in accordance with the law, had been exiled from Athens for 10 years, presumably with family in tow. By 480, however, Xanthippos had been recalled and given command of the Athenian fleet during the war with Persia.

Envisioned as a safety valve by which Athens could protect its political process from malcontents and potential tyrants, ostracism had been introduced some 20 years earlier. By 487, the assembly would vote once each year by a show of hands on the need for an ostracism; if a majority ruled that it was necessary, a second vote would be held about two months later. At that time citizens would scratch the name of anyone they wished to exile onto shards of pottery, or *ostraka*. A count of 6,000 votes against a citizen meant that he had 10 days to pack up and leave the city for a 10-year exile.

That some citizens took poisonous pleasure in the process is evidenced by surviving examples of such ostraka, most of which carry only the names of those to be ostracized. A few are more descriptive, labeling one candidate "accursed," dubbing another a "traitor," and hinting on a third *ostrakon* that the vote was cast as an act of vengeance.

Xanthippos's sin apparently was that of marrying into the wrong political faction, an aristocratic family thought by its enemies to be forever covetous of power. But after

Spectators in the farthest rows of the theater could make out the exaggerated expressions on Greek masks.

Carved into a hillside, this semicircle of tiered seats in the theater at Epidaurus could hold 14,000 spectators.

A DAY AT THE THEATER

For Athenians, theater performances were more than a night out on the town, they were an important part of the festivals of Dionysos, religious celebrations held in honor of the god. Plays were staged at the Theater of Dionysos, near the Acropolis, and were just one element among other festivities that included parades, processions, libations, and sacrifices.

For as many as four days, spectators would sit in the open air, watching the performances taking place on the flat circular area of the theater known as the orchestra. There, each play was presented by three main actors—always men—and by a larger group called the chorus.

By changing masks and costumes, the actors could play several different roles (including those of women), using broad gestures and booming voices in order to reach the whole audience. Meanwhile, the elaborately clad members of the chorus would sing, dance, and address the spectators directly about events in the

play. Should divine intervention be required, an actor playing a god could fly onto the stage with the help of a crane.

The plays were held as dramatic contests, complete with judges, prizes, and award ceremonies for the best actor and playwright. Every year, a city official would choose three playwrights—among the choices would be Sophocles, Euripides, and Aeschylus, the best-known tragedians of the century—to enter the competition. Each writer would present four works. The first three plays were tragedies, their themes usually drawn from the heroic stories of

mythology. Composed in solemn language, these works dealt with human suffering and conflict, and the violent consequences of interaction with the gods. By each play's end—after considerable bloodshed and grief—the troubles usually were resolved.

Each trilogy of tragedies was followed by a so-called satyr play. Performed by actors dressed as satyrs—the half-man, half-animal companions of Dionysos with horses' ears and tails, snub noses, and tousled hair—these plays provided the audience a degree of comic relief, the rowdy and mocking behavior of the satyrs contrast-

ing with the heroic world of the tragedies.

Comedies were also performed at the festivals, with separate prizes for the comedic actors and playwrights. The purpose of Greek comedy was to provide a commentary—sometimes outrageous—on contemporary life. The humor was slapstick and often obscene, and the chorus of the comedy felt free to attack virtually anything and anyone. The plays of the preeminent comic poet, Aristophanes, for example, mocked prominent or eccentric Athenian citizens and delighted in pointing out the absurdity of human behavior.

Masks in hand, the cast assembles before their performance of a satyr play at the sanctuary of Dionysos.

The tragic poet and playwright Euripides *(below, left)* frequently cast women as central, powerful figures in his plays. One such character was Medea, who murdered her own children to exact revenge from her husband; at left, in a scene from the play, Medea stabs her daughter.

Wearing the buffoonish costume of a comic actor, a man holds a torch for a friend visiting his lover in a scene from a play by Aristophanes.

being packed off in disgrace, Xanthippos returned a hero. His son was learning just how fickle a companion public opinion could be. But for the grace of the gods, Pericles now knew, any leader could find himself ostracized, imprisoned, or condemned to death for any indiscretion, perceived or real. Strategoi were particularly vulnerable, since no matter how many victories a general might have to his credit, a single defeat was, in the eyes of many, evidence of criminal conduct.

So far, however, an older, more cautious Pericles had sidestepped such pitfalls, although his building program, of which the Parthenon was only the latest and most ambitious undertaking, was raising some eyebrows. The great temple had taken 10 years to build—10 years and worth every drachma, as far as the general was concerned. And it

In this 19th-century re-creation of the Acropolis, the Parthenon (right), a colossal statue of Athena, and the gateway known as the Propylaia tower over Athens. The buildings' brilliant white marble contrasted vividly with the brightly painted areas.

Lifelike sculptures of high-spirited horses and the Greek gods adorned the exterior of the Parthenon.

would take another six years before the Parthenon's exterior sculptures were completed and painted. These would depict an array of gods and goddesses on the temple's pediments, as well as scenes from mythology—history, in many respects, to the average Athenian—inset in the entablature below the roofline. Inside the colonnade, on the outer walls of the temple, an impressive series of sculptures would capture the pageantry of the Panathenaic festival, the foremost of the city's many religious observances.

Pericles' political enemies pointed to the exorbitant cost of all the new buildings the general had commissioned. Some, according to Plutarch, worried aloud in the assembly that "we are gilding and adorning our city like a wanton woman, dressing it with expensive stones and statues and temples worth millions."

In a free state such as Athens, his critics were certainly entitled to their opinions. But as Pericles scrambled up the steep path that linked the Agora with the Acropolis and paused for a moment to admire the marble Parthenon, it was easy to dismiss such blather as the prattle of the shortsighted and the long wind-

ed. What did they know of duty or of the demands made upon those like himself who were fated to lead, of the unavoidable need, as he saw it, "to know what must be done and to be able to explain it; to love one's country and to be incorruptible."

The general might have been shaken from his reverie by the appearance of his friend, the sculptor Phidias, who was always eager to tell Pericles of the progress that was being made on the Parthenon. Phidias was particularly keen to show off his pet project of the moment—the almost completed statue of the city's patron goddess that stood inside the temple. Passing the dozens of painters and sculptors who continued to work on the building's exterior decorations, the two men loped up the steps of the Parthenon. And for all his self-restraint, Pericles could not keep himself from looking up through its double row of tapered columns, beyond its open doorway, and into the large inner chamber, the cella. The sight was breathtaking. Maybe what people said about Phidias was true after all: Maybe he *had* been given a glimpse of the gods. And maybe, just maybe, as rumor also had it, Phidias had been told to share this knowledge with his fellow Athenians, indeed with all the world.

Inside, Phidias's masterwork, the statue of the goddess Athena, stood 40 feet high. The warrior deity was clad in a tuniclike peplos and a breastplate, and brandished a spear in one hand and a six-foot-tall winged figure of Nike, the goddess of victory, in the other. Her shield and a coiled serpent were at her side. And because the wooden framework of the statue had just recently been plated, Athena's skin was of lustrous ivory and her helmet, armor, and drapery of the brightest gold.

Pericles could only have heaped praise on the sculptor and on his assistants. After strolling through the columned cella, so cool in the midday heat, the two men would have left as they had come, Pericles perhaps pausing again outside to admire the Parthenon anew.

Another statue of a helmeted Athena, this one cast in bronze by Phidias and larger still than the one inside the Parthenon, stood outside on the Acropolis proper. But as Pericles knew, plans were already on the drawing board to give this jewel a suitably monumental setting, in the form of a huge new gateway to be called the Propylaia. Construction was scheduled to get under way next year; in the meantime, sailors off the coast of Attica were already taken with the view of the Acropolis, with the gleaming marble facade of the Parthenon in the foreground and, beyond it, the huge bronze figure of Athena, her gilded helmet shimmering in the sun.

The view from the Acropolis was no less captivating, and Pericles might well have

FOR THE GLORY OF THE GODDESS

According to Greek tradition, the goddess Athena was born in a most unusual way: She sprang from the head of her father, Zeus, "arrayed in arms of war." For the people of Athens nothing less than a spectacular annual festival was due Athena, their guardian deity—to commemorate her birth and to honor the spirit of martial protection that she embodied.

An important festival that was both religious and civic, the Panathenaia took place every year in midsummer, drawing participants from all over Attica for its musical and athletic competitions, ritual procession and sacrifice, and great public feast. Every fourth year a Greater Panathenaia was held, a special thanksgiving celebration that attracted celebrants from the other city-states of Greece.

The first events of the festival were the musical competitions. Professional *kitharodes,* or lyre players and singers, performed in the Odeion, a concert hall built especially for the purpose by Pericles. Poetry reciters called *rhapsodes* declaimed melodiously from the *Iliad* and the *Odyssey,* and flute players, or *auletai,* played distinctive instruments that were said to be an invention of Athena herself. The best performers

Destined for sacrifice to Athena, a bull is led to the altar during the high point of the Panathenaia. A replica of the Parthenon's gold- and ivory-clad statue of Athena in battle dress stands ready to protect her city *(far left)*.

received gilded olive-leaf wreaths and cash prizes as awards.

Athletic contests were the next order of business. The events themselves—footracing, boxing, wrestling, and others—were similar to those put on at the athletic festivals such as the crown games, but the prizes at the Panathenaia were much more valuable. In addition to a victor's wreath, for example, first- and second-place winners received as many as 50 specially commissioned amphorae, each of which held over 10 gallons of olive oil pressed from the fruit of trees in Athena's sacred grove. Other events displayed a martial bent, such as a dance that featured armed men performing to the accompaniment of the double flute. Another was the so-called Contest in Manly Excellence, unique to Athens, in which teams of warriors were evaluated for their size and strength.

After the competitions, the end of the festival was marked by a grand procession of men, women, children, and beasts through the city up to the Acropolis and the precincts of Athena's own temple, the Parthenon *(background, previous page)*, and a smaller temple, the Erechtheion *(background, this page)*. There, a rectangular woolen cloth known as a peplos—woven by a group of matrons specifically for the occasion—was presented to a roughly life-size wooden cult statue of Athena, probably housed in the Erechtheion. Next, a hundred or more bulls were slaughtered on the goddess's altar, located at the highest point on the Acropolis rock, near the Parthenon; the bones and fat of the animals were left as a burnt offering while the citizenry feasted on the meat. By these gifts the people of Athens paid their respects to Athena and could be assured of her protection for another year.

A priest accepts from a young girl a newly woven peplos, the gown that will clothe one of the statues of Athena on the Acropolis. Depicted on the peplos was a scene of the goddess battling giants.

The figure of an athlete at the top of his form adorned a prize amphora for the winning discus thrower at the Panathenaia.

A scene on a Panathenaic amphora shows a singer and a flutist performing for judges during the festival's music competition.

stopped to look down on the city that was his world and on the ring of bright water, which, thanks to the Athenian navy, protected that world as effectively as any moat. From here, too, he could easily have seen the city walls and, punctuating the landscape within, the craggy outcrops of the Areopagus, where a court that tried cases of homicide met in a rock-cut gallery, and the Pnyx, meeting place of the assembly. The land beyond Athens's ramparts was much like the land inside the city itself—rocky, rumpled by hills and mountains, the soil so thin and parched that although it was possible for farmers to grow wheat, they focused most of their efforts on vines and drought-resistant olives. Years later Plato would compare Attica to "the skeleton of a body wasted by disease; the rich soft soil has all run away leaving the land nothing but skin and bone."

On such skin and bone, however, Athens had seen fit to build an empire, and on a day not far off Pericles would have cause to count for his countrymen the ways in which "our city is worthy of admiration." The proof of that lay before him. To the northwest, straddling the

For whenever I look at you for a moment,
then nothing comes to me to say,
but my tongue is frozen in silence,
straightway a subtle flame has run under my skin,
I see nothing with my eyes,
and my ears are buzzing . . . a little short of death
I seem in my distraught wits.

Panathenaic Way, lay the Agora, somewhat quieter now in the doldrums of early afternoon, and around it the government buildings to which he would shortly return. If he
was so inclined, Pericles could pick out other neighborhoods—the working-class dis-
tricts on the other side of the Agora, for example, or the potters' workshops surrounding the Temple of Hephaistos, or even the Street of the Marbleworkers, stretching southwest from the Agora.

Here and elsewhere throughout Athens stood houses and workshops in the hundreds, their walls built of unbaked brick, their angled roofs set with tiles of terra cotta.
Among them, too, was Pericles' own home, as modest as the
rest. Under all those roofs lived and worked the best that
Greece had to offer, Pericles reflected proudly, rich and
poor alike, honorable all, "for the love of honor," as he
well knew, "is the only thing which does not grow old."

It would have been pleasant to linger there,
gazing out across the city, especially with the sun
so warm on his back, the sky so blue, and the
wind so soft off the Aegean. But, he reminded himself, there was an afternoon's work yet to be done,
and so reluctantly he
turned to retrace his
steps to the Ago-
ra and the build-
ings where the busi-
ness of Athens was
conducted.

Looking off to his left as he descended, Pericles
would have seen a pair of parallel walls as impenetrable as those that embraced the city. These were the so-
called Long Walls that extended from the far side of the
ring wall. Forming both a corridor and an economic life-
line, the walls traveled southwest some five miles to the
outer ramparts of Piraeus, Athens's commercial window on
the Aegean Sea and home port to the empire's formidable
fleet. Piraeus was also home to many Athenian metics, the

foreigners who had taken up permanent residence in the state. Among them was a man named Kephalos, who at some time during the 430s BC had left his native Sicily to begin a new life in the city of Athens.

Ever since he arrived, Kephalos had thrived in his adopted home. He had established there a successful shield factory and over the years had become friends with various leaders of Athenian society. Like the good metic that he was, he had been diligent in fulfilling his responsibilities as a resident alien, registering as a foreigner, paying the special metic tax every year, and otherwise abiding by the laws of his adopted country. Moreover, as his factory prospered and his wealth accumulated, Kephalos took on a number of additional duties that were ordinarily the province of citizens, and well-to-do ones at that. Chief among these tasks were the so-called liturgies, or the private funding of such public works as plays, festivals, and athletic contests. Like wealthier citizens, too, he paid property tax, an indication that unlike most of his fellow metics he had been granted by the assembly the right to own property. For all that, however, there was little prospect that he or his family members would ever be made citizens, the only people who had any say in the political life of the Athenian state.

At the time, Kephalos would have been but one of some 25,000 metics living in Athens and Piraeus—most, like the shieldmaker himself, attracted by economic opportunity. Indeed, his own investment in the shield factory had paid off beyond his most optimistic expectations. No other Athenian factory had more workers, for example, although the dozens of slaves who shouldered most of the labor would hardly have considered themselves employees. And his own substantial income only underscored what everyone in Athens already believed: that while citizens owned the land and held the public offices and the power that went with them, metics had a tight grip on the city's economy.

Not that this accepted state of affairs caused any resentment. To the contrary, metics were more than welcome in Athens, where most citizens shared the opinion of the dramatist Aristophanes that just as the heartiest bread is a mixture of flour and bran, the healthiest city is composed of more refined citizens and coarser metics. Besides, as the bran of Athens, metics freed citizens from much of the drudgery associated with daily life, leaving citizens with more free time in which to participate in their democracy.

Kephalos's fellow metics represented a cross section of the Athenian economy. Ordinary laborers, skilled artisans, and successful entrepreneurs like himself were all, often as not, metics. So, too, were many of the peddlers and moneychangers who could be found in the Agora on most mornings of the week, as well as some of the empire's most influential traders and bankers. And metics were equally well represented in the arts and sciences: Hippocrates and Herodotus, for example, respectively the fathers of medicine and history, were metics, as was the philosopher Anaxagoras, who had been mentor to Pericles when he was a young man.

In Piraeus, at least, it was almost a given that most of the people on the streets were metics, and Kephalos in the course of his day's work would undoubtedly have come into contact with many of his kind. Yet unless he knew them personally, he would have had a hard time identifying any one of them as a metic. Unlike true foreigners, Athens-born and -raised metics dressed no differently than citizens, or some slaves for that matter, and metics spoke to citizens as their equals; they even earned as much as citizens for the same work.

As in Athens, things got off to an early start in Piraeus, so that Aristophanes' description of the scene in the former was no less true of the latter. "As soon as the cock sends forth his morning song," he wrote, "they all jump out of bed, blacksmiths, potters, leather-dressers, shoe-makers, bathmen, flour-dealers, lyre-turners and shield-makers; they slip on their shoes and rush off to their work in the dark."

In his prime Kephalos would have been among them, hurrying from home along Piraeus's new gridwork of wide streets, so easily navigated compared with the narrow, congested alleys of Athens. With the smell of the nearby sea in his nostrils and the sounds of sea gulls chattering in his ears, he would have stepped past the homes of shipowners and bankers, every now and then catching a glimpse of the big freighters in the harbor and the rows of porticoed warehouses opposite the wharves.

Those ships, some long and narrow and bristling with oars, others round-built and sporting a single sail, helped make Piraeus the emporium of the entire eastern Mediterranean. Grain flowed in from ports along the Black Sea; timber from Macedonia; linen and exotic animals from Egypt; carpets from Carthage; bronzes from Etruria; perfumes from Arabia; as well as ivory, wool, wine, cheese, and many other commodities from points east and west. Small wonder, then, that Pericles could boast of Athens that "the greatness of our city attracts, one after the other, the products of the whole world."

Kephalos's own world revolved around his factory, and ducking now into its doorway and pressing the door shut behind him, he may well have sunk into a chair to catch his breath, savoring the silence for a moment before the clatter of tools and metal echoed again through the building. It wasn't long, in fact, before the first of his workers slipped into the shop to begin a day that wouldn't end until sunset, some 14 hours later. By then, too, many of his craftsmen would have lowered their tunics to their waists in the heat of the day; a few would be working in the nude, with only caps to catch their sweat.

As far as we know, all of these workers were slaves, and many other factories in Piraeus and Athens also made use of slave labor. Few factories, however, were anywhere near as large as Kephalos's, although a factory of any size was hardly typical of Athenian industry. Instead, most goods were manufactured in small, family-run workshops, many of which were passed from one generation to the next.

Kephalos was himself hoping that at least one of his four sons would keep the factory in the family. Even so, he realized that not every son would want to follow in a father's footsteps, and that today, more than when he was a young man, so many other professions seemed attractive. Lysias, with his flair for language, might want to become a speechwriter, Polemarchus a doctor, Euthydemus a grain dealer, Brachyllus a banker. Accordingly, Kephalos was giving his sons the best education that the empire had to offer, as good an education, in fact, as the sons of any citizen received.

For his part, there must have been times when Kephalos could not resist wandering around his own factory, ostensibly to oversee the work, but mostly to savor all that he had done. Watching the raw metal take shape at the forge, staring absentmindedly into the flames, still flinching after all these years as muscled arms, glistening with sweat, swung hammers heavily against anvils, Kephalos could recall the early days of building the business, when he had been worried about whether he could ever generate enough orders to make good on his investment. Admiring the smooth efficiency with which his shieldmakers went about their work, he could remember how difficult it had been over the years to build such a well-oiled operation. Now, seeing so many finished shields stacked shining in the storeroom,

Linked to Athens by the Long Walls *(center, background)*, the town of Piraeus served both as the city's port and as headquarters for its fleet. Piraeus, which boasted three heavily fortified harbors, was also an important industrial center, home to many artisans, like the helmetmaker below.

he was filled with a real sense of pride in his own accomplishments.

Still, Kephalos had his regrets, and none greater than the citizenship that had eluded him so far and seemed destined to elude his sons as well. Yet according to the way he looked at it, being a metic was more or less a contract: If you worked hard and played by the rules, not only would success attend you, but Athens would look after you. And while it wasn't something that he liked to dwell on, since it so rarely happened, he knew that there was always the chance that if he worked hard and enjoyed more than his share of luck, a vote of the assembly might just reward him with citizenship.

Kephalos's hopes were to come to naught, however. Of all of his sons, Lysias would be the most successful, going on to become a well-regarded *logographos,* a kind of shadow lawyer; indeed, by most accounts he was the best logographos of his day, as adept with his stylus as Pericles was with his tongue. But neither talent nor fame brought citizenship any closer to Lysias than loyalty had to Kephalos, and both father and son would die as they had lived—proud residents of Athens but metics to the last.

At the end of a long day, the Athenian most responsible for the city's restrictive citizenship law had finished his work in and around the Agora and was on his way home. There, on the doorstep, Pericles was met by the ravishing Aspasia. Lifting herself on the tips of her toes, her peplos exposing both ankles, Aspasia met Pericles kiss for kiss. As anyone who had ever seen them embrace knew, she had never made a secret of her love for the man that she considered her husband, and she was not about to start. In fact, as a former *hetaira,* a kind of high-class courtesan, she had never made a secret of her affection, brief though it might have been, for any man.

But that was then, and now she was the consort of the most powerful man in

Athens and the mother of their two-year-old son. Nevertheless, the cream of Athenian society had never quite forgiven Aspasia her past, even if, in setting up housekeeping with Pericles, she had raised her status from socially acceptable hetaira to socially respectable *pallake,* or concubine. For in a society that expected women to be seldom seen and rarely heard, she was the good wife's worst nightmare: Aspasia was witty, intelligent, sexually alluring, defiantly independent, and owing to her status as a metic, liberated from the strictures that kept some females housebound.

Aspasia paid a price for such effrontery, of course. Scandalmongers whispered that she continued to associate with courtesans and even went so far as to procure other women for her notoriously oversexed husband, satirists lampooned her as a "dog-eyed whore," and her husband's political rivals saw in Aspasia a means by which to undermine his authority. And yet, as any man or woman who had met her could attest, to share even a conversation with so incandescent a presence was to fall immediately under her spell.

To be sure, the distinction between a hetaira and a pal-

Renowned for her intelligence and her political astuteness, Pericles' common-law wife, Aspasia, moved in a world that was considered off-limits to most of the women of her day.

84

lake was not lost on those discriminating Athenians who went to the trouble of categorizing both their erotic pleasures and the women who provided them. No Athenian, for example, would ever have frowned upon a man who kept company with a courtesan, nor have batted an eye had the same man brought that same woman home as his personal concubine. But to do as Pericles had done and to give such a woman, and a metic at that, the respect due only a wife—that was unforgivable in the eyes of those not given to forgiveness. After all, said one Athenian who evidently had his priorities straight, "We have courtesans for pleasure, concubines to perform our domestic chores, and wives to bear us legitimate children and be the faithful guardians of our homes."

In addition to the prohibition on marrying a citizen, Aspasia the metic would have found herself subject to all the other restrictions faced by non-Athenian-born residents. On the other hand, metics were free to make a living as they pleased, just as Kephalos had done in Piraeus. For some metic women, that meant putting domestic skills to profitable use as weavers, cobblers, and seamstresses. For others, such as Aspasia, it was perhaps too tempting to trade on more innate talents. Setting herself up as a hetaira, Aspasia, gift of the "goddess of lust," as one Greek poet mockingly described her, succeeded so well that she reportedly opened her own brothel and taught other young women the seductive arts that made a hetaira as desirable for her graciousness as for her body.

"We have courtesans for pleasure, concubines to perform our domestic chores, and wives to bear us legitimate children."

That Pericles could only treat Aspasia as his wife and not actually marry her was the unhappy result of an old law that forbade marriage between citizens and metics. To make matters worse for Aspasia, she had also had the ill fortune to arrive in Athens sometime after 451 BC, after Pericles' new law denying citizenship to the children of such liaisons had gone into effect. When she arrived in Athens, Aspasia was probably in her middle or late teens, of marriageable age by Athenian standards. By some accounts, she had even come to Athens from Miletus in the eastern Aegean with the express intention of finding a husband. If so, she could never have imagined how lucky in love she would be, nor foreseen that the man who would win her heart could never legally become her husband.

But while there were many hetairai in Athens, there was only one Aspasia. She was, in fact, that rarest of women in Athens: the social equal of any man. No other woman, it was said, made a man feel more like the self-important animal he could be. And no other woman could so hold her own in the company of men, that even as demanding a conversationalist as Socrates eagerly engaged her in dialogue and brought along his students to share the rhetorical fireworks.

Such was Aspasia's celebrity that Pericles would likely have heard of her before he met her. Eyes always followed her in the Agora, where hers was a familiar figure, her hair fashionably frizzed and piled atop her head. And she was equally welcome in the *symposia,* those otherwise all-male and wine-fueled banquets, where her keen intellect was appreciated no less than her wit and her charm.

And then at some time in the 440s BC, Aspasia did meet Pericles, whether by design, as her less generous critics claimed, or by the happenstance of fate. Either way, it was Pericles who was swept off his feet. In what must have seemed no time at all, the middle-aged statesman—by now divorced from his first wife—had cast aside any concern for public opinion and had made a mistress of a woman who could never be his wife.

This, then, was the Aspasia who leaned into Pericles as he left his home each morning and again when he returned at the end of the workday and who, on many an evening, might have strolled arm in arm with him through the columned courtyard of their home and into their living room. On many evenings, too, both might later have lingered over dinner, discussing the

weightier issues of the day by the flickering glow of an oil lamp. But on this particular evening their time together would have been briefer than usual if Aspasia planned later that night to attend one of the symposia that she so enjoyed.

As was often the case with such affairs, this symposium was probably thrown by a friend on the spur of the moment. Pericles would usually have been invited along to the banquet too, of course. But invariably the general would politely decline, choosing instead to spend a few hours alone. This would not prevent the more social Aspasia from attending, however: Welcoming the chance to get together with friends and join in what was sure to be a lively discussion, she would frequently go alone.

Since the typical Athenian rose early and went to bed early, most social activities took place during the daytime. Not surprisingly, given their raucous reputation, symposia were the one notable exception to this rule, as these usually began after sunset and

In this symposium scene, one man drinks wine, another flings his dregs in the game known as *kottabos,* and a third plays the lyre.

might easily drag on into the small hours of the morning. Accordingly, Aspasia would have arrived at the home of her host shortly after dark. Once inside, she would have removed her sandals before entering the andron—the room set aside for the master of the house and the usual setting for a symposium—and had her feet washed by one of the host's servants.

Aspasia could be forgiven for not noticing the room itself, so alike were the settings for all symposia. Almost certainly the couches were laid out in the usual manner, an arrangement that allowed the feasters to recline comfortably, two to a couch, and easily converse with one another. The floor, usually tiled, unlike the earthen floors in the rest of the house, probably included a drain that made it easier for the servants to mop up the mess and wash away the debris once everyone had gone home. Toward the same end, the master's dogs were allowed to roam freely during the symposium. That way, discarded bones and scraps of food would be devoured as fast as the symposiasts tossed them to the floor. So, too, would all the chunks of bread that the revelers used as napkins, as forks were unknown in Athens and food was eaten with the fingers.

Aspasia would also have thought nothing of the absence of women at these drinking parties, since with rare exceptions, herself among them, a symposium was strictly for men; the only other women present were those who had been hired for the night, either to entertain the men or to seduce them, or both. Socrates himself—no slouch at a symposium and capable of drinking most guests under the table—was at one memorable symposium in which a young couple acted out Dionysos's seduction of Ariadne, daughter of the king of Crete. According to one chronicler, the pair performed so wantonly and with such carnal effect on the merrymakers that "the bachelor guests swore they would marry at the first opportunity, while the husbands present left the party on horseback at full gallop, intent on a joyous reunion with their wives."

At its simplest, of course, a symposium was a discussion, and so long as the guests were only eating and not drinking, talk did reign and Aspasia would have had the chance to show off her much-vaunted erudition. But once the food had been cleared away, the guests would have donned garlands on their heads and the host—dubbed the "leader of the drinking," or the symposiarch—would have mixed the first krater of wine and water in anticipation of the tippling that was the evening's main event. After that, the activities of a symposium were best summed up in a drinking song of the time: "Drink with me, play music with me, love with me, wear a crown with me, be mad with me when I am mad and wise with me when I am wise."

Most of the women at symposia were either entertainers or prostitutes. At left, a woman comforts a reveler who has overindulged.

Before taking the dose of hemlock that would end his life, Socrates converses with followers about his fearless welcoming of death. Socrates was condemned to die for "refusing to recognize the gods of the state" and for "corrupting the youth."

Whether mad or wise, Socrates, Aspasia, and their fellow revelers would have presented the opening drinks of the evening as a sacrifice, or libation, to the gods. Often this early round was sipped from saucer-shaped cups; but for the rest of the evening's drinking, these small cups would have been replaced by larger goblets called kylikes or even by flagon-sized drinking horns. Flute girls, dancers, and hetairai may have worked the room, offering their respective services, while the guests themselves took turns singing or reciting poetry, or did their best to sustain the earlier topic of discussion. Periodically, the symposiasts would have engaged in the popular game of *kottabos*, testing their accuracy—not to mention their sobriety—by flinging the dregs of their wine at an agreed-upon target.

At some point in the evening's festivities, perhaps even before the last round and a final libation to the god Hermes, Aspasia may well have called it a night. A servant would have helped her back into her sandals, and donning her woolen cloak and pulling its folds tightly to her chest, she would have stepped into the night and hurried home to Pericles.

But the fact that Aspasia had been out at all would only heighten the resentment that some felt toward her. Other wives, including the wives of the men at the symposium, all of them good women in the eyes of Athenian society, had been in their beds for hours. And none would ever have dared to attend a symposium, let alone to have voiced an opinion on whatever subject had been discussed that night. Aspasia, however, could do as she pleased, talk as she pleased, and, it was rumored, bend Pericles as she pleased, even in matters of politics— things that were no wife's business, let alone a mistress's.

Writing long after the fact, Plutarch would claim that Pericles had courted Aspasia specifically "because of her wisdom and skill in politics," although he did admit that there had been an erotic element to their relationship as well. Plutarch further remarked that Aspasia took as her role model Thargelia, a courtesan from Asia Minor who in her day—about 50 years before—had sought to win the hearts of the high and mighty in order to enslave their minds and influence their politics.

Many in Athens would have had no trouble believing such things about Aspasia. As a matter of fact, two years earlier, in 440 BC, when Athens sided with the Milesians in a dispute between Aspasia's native Miletus and its neighboring island of Samos, the word was that his mistress had once again worked her wiles on Pericles, and blame for the war was laid at her shapely feet. More than ever, there were those who wanted Aspasia out of the way. But with Pericles' popularity at its peak after his defeat of the Samians, they opted first for a softer target.

The sculptor Phidias, still basking in the acclaim showered upon him for his work on the Parthenon, would have seemed unlikely prey. He was a friend of Pericles, however, and a successful case against Phidias might well expose any weakness in the general's standing with the people. Moreover, the sculptor appeared to have made a potentially costly error in including, so it was rumored, his own image on the shield of his statue of Athena. Then he had gone on to trump that sacrilege by similarly slipping in a likeness of Pericles.

The general's enemies were quick to exploit the opportunity thus presented. No sooner was his Athena completed and dedicated in

Socrates' student Plato *(left)* "gave thanks to nature, first that he was born a human being rather than a dumb animal; second that he was a man rather than a woman; then that he was a Greek not a foreigner; finally that he was Athenian born in the time of Socrates."

89

438 than Phidias was charged with impiety and, for good measure, with the embezzlement of some of the gold intended for the statue. The latter accusation was groundless, and the sculptor, with the help of Pericles, easily proved it so. The charge of impiety stuck, though, and he was sentenced to exile.

Emboldened, Pericles' enemies next pressed their attack against his old teacher, Anaxagoras, and against Aspasia. In the case of the former, a bill was introduced in the assembly, as Plutarch explained, "providing for the public impeachment of such as did not believe in gods, or who taught doctrines regarding the heavens." The target of the bill, obvious to anyone who knew him, was the none-too-pious philosopher, who had long ago helped Pericles free himself from the shackles of superstition. Sensing the danger, Pericles encouraged Anaxagoras to leave Athens without delay.

At that time Pericles was in full command of strategy, and he continued to lead Athens at the beginning of the war. In the winter of the following year he delivered his funeral oration over the first Athenians to fall in the conflict, reminding his audience of the forebears who had given them freedom and empire, of the greatness of their city, and of the sacrifice of the dead.

But as a result of the crowding in of the countrymen when the Spartans attacked Attica, a plague began to ravage Athens in 430 BC, claiming many of its citizens and severely damaging the morale of the rest. For the first time the general failed to persuade the people to follow his policies; his speeches fell on less responsive ears, and he may have heard the catcalls and whistles that would become all too familiar in the assembly in the years ahead. It was during this crisis that the enemies of the general struck: A bill was put

"Be mad with me when I am mad and wise with me when I am wise."

Aspasia proved less slippery in avoiding her day in court. Also charged with impiety, she was brought to trial, and the case against her was bolstered by the further accusation that she had procured freeborn women for her supposedly insatiable common-law husband. Pericles took the stand on her behalf and, in Plutarch's words, secured her acquittal by pleading shamelessly with the jurors and "by shedding copious tears."

Having tasted blood, however, Pericles' adversaries prepared to close in for the kill: This time their quarry was the general himself. But by now war was looming between Athens and her southern neighbor Sparta, and following a succession of crises between these two most powerful of Greek city-states, fighting broke out in 431 BC.

forth and quickly passed that Pericles' public accounts should be audited, in the hope that a close scrutiny would provide grounds for some charge, any charge, whether of embezzlement, bribery, or simple malfeasance. The "first citizen" stood trial before the assembly and was sentenced to a big fine and dismissed from his generalship. His fellow citizens did elect him again to the post in 429, but he passed away shortly after reentering office, another victim of the plague.

The man who had ushered in the Athenian golden age was gone, and the fate of the city—its democracy, its wealth, its influence in the world—had been turned over to the men of war. But after more than a half-century of success on the field of battle, Athens was confident of victory.

THE AGE OF HEROES

Tales of the exploits and miraculous feats of heroes permeated Greek life. A youth's education consisted, in large measure, of reading and memorizing the epic poems that told of heroic figures such as Theseus, Agamemnon, Achilles, Herakles, and Odysseus. When these young men grew older and attended the social get-togethers known as symposia, they would be entertained by dramatic recitations of these tales by *rhapsodes (left)* or they might simply take turns retelling the stories themselves.

Everyone knew the fantastic voyages, epic battles, and wondrous adventures of the characters from Homer's *Iliad* and *Odyssey* and Hesiod's *Theogony,* or *Birth of the Gods.* But these and other narratives represented more than just entertainment for the Greeks; they were looked on as models for right living. Heroes were handsome, strong, and courageous. They were respectful and protective of the weak and the poor. Though they had human failings, heroes embodied the concepts of honor, nobility, and perseverance.

Their tales inspired and encouraged Greek youths who had yet to experience battle, renewed the spirit of a warrior in his prime, and reminded the aged veteran of his fallen comrades. The stories of the heroes instilled in men the meaning of duty and the desire for glory worthy of notice by the gods themselves.

Lyre in hand, Theseus *(near right)* leads the Athenian maidens and youths to Crete to face the Minotaur.

LOYAL THESEUS

A prince of Crete was murdered while visiting in Attica, and as punishment, the city of Athens was under a dreadful obligation: Every nine years it had to send seven youths and seven maidens to the island kingdom, where they faced death at the hands of a horrible monster. The Minotaur, half man and half bull, awaited his victims in the dark recesses of the mazelike Labyrinth under the palace of King Minos.

But one year, as the time for the next sacrifice drew near, Athenians had reason to hope for deliverance from their terrible covenant. A hero named Theseus, after conducting a long crusade to rid the countryside of murderous bandits, was reunited with his father, Aegeus, the Athenian king. Theseus offered to lead the delegation to Crete and fight the Minotaur as proof of his commitment to the city of his father.

In hand-to-hand combat, Theseus killed the beast, thus saving the lives of the Athenian youths. Moreover, the legends say that after succeeding his father on the throne, the young hero redefined the role of the king and established representative councils, demonstrating through these actions that his loyalty to Athens—his *polis,* or city-state—was paramount. In so doing, Theseus set an example that eventually led Greeks to swear primary allegiance to their polis instead of to their clan.

Theseus slays the half-man, half-bull found in the depths of King Minos's palace at Knossos, Crete *(opposite).*

93

Fashioned from a single sheet of hammered gold, the burial mask of a Mycenaean king *(above)* reveals a fearsome beauty. At left, regal lions form the pediment over the main gate to the Mycenaean citadel. Though Agamemnon believed he had killed his daughter, it was said that Artemis whisked her away at the last moment, leaving a deer in her place *(right)*.

AGAMEMNON, MARSHAL OF ARMIES

Trouble was brewing in Sparta: King Tyndareus had to select a husband for his daughter, Helen, known far and wide as the most beautiful woman in the world. Hot-blooded kings from every corner of Greece crowded into his palace and were on the verge of coming to blows. Luckily, Tyndareus's other daughter was already married to Agamemnon, the king of Mycenae, who offered a solution: To prevent bloodshed, all the suitors should vow to support and defend the man who won Helen's hand. Menelaus, Agamemnon's brother, was the fortunate man to take Helen as his bride, but his good fortune was short lived. Thanks to some divine meddling by Aphrodite, the Trojan prince Paris seduced Helen and spirited her away to his fortress city across the Aegean.

This insult brought a fierce response. Reminding the Greek kings of their promise, Agamemnon gathered an army to punish Troy and retrieve Helen. Over many months, he called on the greatest warriors of Greece—Ajax, Diomedes, Odysseus, and Achilles—and all agreed to join the quest. But first, the oracles had to be consulted, and they delivered frightful tidings: To provide the wind needed to carry the Greek army to Troy, the goddess Artemis demanded the sacrifice of Agamemnon's daughter, Iphigeneia. Agamemnon was devastated, but, conscious of his responsibility as king, he put duty ahead of his feelings. When the maiden came to the altar, the assembled warriors wept at her willingness to die for their cause. They looked away as her father struck her with the sacrificial knife. The Trojan War had claimed its first victim.

THE GLORY OF ACHILLES

Troy finally fell when Greek warriors were smuggled inside the city walls in a hollow horse.

As Homer's epic poem of the Trojan War opens, the Greeks' fiercest warrior is sitting in his tent sulking. Achilles, son of the Myrmidon king Peleus and the sea nymph Thetis, was grievously insulted when Agamemnon, commander of the Greek army, took from Achilles his prize from a previous battle, a woman named Briseis. As a result, the hero withdrew from the fighting, watching indifferently as the Trojans repelled each and every Greek assault.

At long last, Achilles was roused to battle by a fresh anger that replaced the old one. Achilles' beloved friend, Patroklos, had gone to battle in his stead and was slain by Troy's hero, Hector. Thetis had long ago prophesied Achilles' fate: He could enjoy a long life of peaceful pursuits or he could take the field of battle with the certain knowledge that he would die. To Achilles, and to Greeks of later generations who heard this story, the choice was clear: Great men should seek a life covered in glory no matter how short it might be. Achilles did meet his end at Troy—felled by an arrow in the heel, his one weak point—but his legend lives on.

Fired by a desire for vengeance, Achilles lunges at Hector, Troy's noblest warrior. The ruins of the once splendid Trojan city are embedded in a hill in modern-day Turkey (far right).

Odysseus clings to the belly of a ram *(below)* to escape the cave of the Cyclops, Polyphemos. While his men plugged their ears with wax, Odysseus tied himself to the mast *(right)* to resist the Sirens, whose songs enticed sailors into dashing their ships upon the rocks. Upon his return to Ithaca *(far right)* Odysseus regained his throne and his faithful wife, Penelope.

WILY ODYSSEUS

In the stories of the Trojan War and its aftermath, one character appears time and again. Odysseus, king of Ithaca, was a different type of hero—one who could use his head as well as brute force to win the day. After the fall of Troy, Odysseus and his companions set sail for home. But the sea god, Poseidon, summoned storms and earthquakes that swept them off course. They wandered the western seas and visited lands of strange customs and fearsome inhabitants. Odysseus outsmarted the one-eyed monster, the Cyclops, and eluded capture by the Sirens. He was detained by the enchantress Circe and the goddess Calypso, both of whom offered him a life of bliss. He even visited the land of the dead and spoke with the spirit of his comrade, Achilles. For all the wonder and terror, however, he kept one goal in mind: to return home. Finally, after 20 years, Odysseus reached the shores of Ithaca, only to find his palace overtaken by suitors vying for the hand of his wife, Penelope. Through a combination of guile and strength, Odysseus and his son—grown to manhood in his absence—slaughtered those who had violated the sacred bonds of hospitality. By the conclusion of the *Odyssey,* the hero has completed his task: Honor has been served, glory won, and the household restored to harmony and order.

HERAKLES, SON OF ZEUS

Throughout all of Greece, there was one hero who stood above all others for the magnitude of his exploits. Herakles was the child of the god Zeus and a mortal queen, Alkmene, at whose court he received a warrior's training to supplement his brash self-confidence.

To atone for murders he had committed while under the spell of Zeus's jealous wife, Hera, Herakles submitted himself to the service of King Eurystheus. The king gave Herakles 12 seemingly impossible labors, each more arduous than the last. He strangled a lion whose skin was impenetrable by sword or spear; he supported the world on his shoulders while the Titan Atlas retrieved golden apples from his daughters; he journeyed to the underworld and returned with its guardian, Cerberus, in tow.

For these feats and many others, Herakles won fame and admiration among both gods and men. When death was about to claim him, Zeus conferred immortality upon Herakles and brought him to Olympus, where he was ever after worshiped as a god. For a hero, there was no greater reward.

For his last labor, Herakles captured Cerberus, guardian of the underworld, and brought the beast to the mist-shrouded mountains of his homeland in the Peloponnesos *(left)*.

CHAPTER THREE

SWORDS AND PLOWSHARES

A helmet hammered from a single sheet of bronze and a two-part piece of armor called a cuirass encased the head, chest, and back of Greek hoplite warriors. A successful campaign also employed archers, javelin throwers, and cavalry, but the heavily equipped infantrymen formed the backbone of the armies of fifth-century-BC Greece.

F or the farmers who made up the solidly dependable middle class of Athenian society, it was a familiar ritual in the annual round of hard work. Just as the grain harvest took place in June, the vintage in September, the sowing of barley seed in October, and the gathering of olives in November, so, too, practically every summer came the call to a different kind of labor: the defense of the homeland.

Heeding the call, the Athenian farmer would haul down from its customary place above the hearth his cumbersome and soot-blackened combat gear: body armor, helmet, shield, sword, and spear. His wife or slave would clean and polish the weapons and equipment, and pack it all in leather bags. A few days' rations of barley groats, cheese, olives, onions, and wine would be tossed into another sack, to which the pungent odor of stale onions always clung as a reminder of previous campaigns. Then, together with his slave, his brothers, and his friends and neighbors, he would turn his back on his farm and march off to war.

By the end of the fifth century BC, some kind of military service was required from virtually every male in Athens—citizen, metic, and slave—between the ages of 18 and 60. The type of service varied with economic standing, however. The wealthiest men, for example, rode in a small cavalry corps or served as ship captains. The lowest class in Athens, the *thetes,* would fight as archers and javelin throwers. And thetes and slaves would also take their places at the oars that powered the long, graceful warships of the growing fleet.

But during the first decade or so of the century, the defense of Athens rested almost entirely upon the brawny shoulders of the heavily armored infantrymen referred to as hoplites, or "those who provide their own shields." These were the farmers and other members of the middle class who could afford the elaborate fighting equipment that cost about 30 drachmas—the equivalent of six fine oxen—along with a personal servant to lug the 70 pounds of gear. Their name derived from the *hoplon,* the round, three-foot shield that each one carried. Hoplites were true citizen-soldiers: They had few professional officers, lacked regular uniforms or elaborate medals, and collected no pay.

In battle the hoplites would advance en masse in a formation known as the phalanx

In preparation for battle, a warrior wearing a helmet with a crest of horsehair dons the bronze leg protectors called greaves *(far left),* while his mate fastens a heavy linen tunic. The two soldiers at right make last-minute adjustments to sword and hair.

and fight the enemy at the closest range possible. "Toe to toe and shield against shield hard-driven," as one Greek poet put it, "crest against crest and helmet on helmet, chest against chest."

Greek warfare was a highly ritualized form of limited combat. It typically consisted of one brutal and decisive battle bereft of individual heroics, and it was often brief enough to take the farmer away from his chores for only a few days at a time. Moreover, phalanx warfare required little in the way of formal training or tactical brilliance, demanding instead the same muscular strength, physical endurance, and iron nerve needed to eke a living from the stone-studded Greek earth. It was, said one chronicler, "a sweet thing to him who does not know it, but to him who has made trial of it, it is a thing of fear."

An unusual call to arms—to this "thing of fear"—came in 490 BC. But the transgressor was not one of the neighboring Greek states with which the Athenians periodically warred. This time it was a foreign invader from across the Aegean Sea. In July of that year the Persians, who already controlled most of the Near East, dispatched a 600-ship fleet toward the east coast of Greece. Aboard were their crack units of archers and cavalrymen, as well as regular foot soldiers, over 20,000 men in all. Also on board was an 80-year-old Greek named Hippias, the former tyrant of Athens who hoped that the Persians would restore him to power. It was Hippias who guided the Persians to a location where the abilities of their cavalry could be exploited to the full. The place he chose was a narrow coastal plain hemmed in by mountains and sea, some 26 miles northeast of Athens: The battle would be fought on the plain of Marathon.

Even before the Persians set foot on the Greek mainland, hoplites in and around Athens began mobilizing for war. Muster rolls listing the citizens to be called up were posted in the city's marketplace, the Agora. Then the Athenian army—some 10,000 strong—set out on the eight-hour trek to Marathon.

Nearing the plain, the Athenians set up camp at some distance from the Persian army, which had spread out near the beach. There the Athenians were joined by about 1,000 hoplites from their northern neighbor Plataea. But they expected more reinforcements; specifically, a contingent of hoplites from Athens's ally to the south, Sparta.

While the Athenians waited for word of the Spartans, there was another reason for a delay of battle: the presence of too many commanders on the ground. Athens's 10 generals, or *strategoi,* who were elected annually by the assembly of the people, were all at Marathon. Also present was Callimachus, an official known as the *polemarch,* who served as the nominal commander in chief. In battle, Callimachus sometimes deferred to his generals—when they could make up their minds, that is. But at Marathon the top brass debated whether to attack the Persians immediately or wait for help from Sparta—and wound up hopelessly divided.

Finally, one of the generals, a man named Miltiades, managed to gain the ear of Callimachus. An old aristocratic swashbuckler in his sixties, Miltiades was evidently the only general with firsthand experience of the Persians. Although he was Athenian by birth, he had spent much of his life ruling the family fiefdom in the northern Aegean, located at a vital strategic position guarding access to the Black Sea. Then, in 493 BC, the Persians had come, and he had been forced to flee to Athens. And now, three years later, he faced them again. On this occasion, however, Miltiades was determined to fight—and to do so without any further delay.

Speaking to his superior, Callimachus, the wily old general marshaled his most persuasive arguments. "Athens has never faced as great a danger as that which threatens her now," he declared, according to the historian Herodotus. "If the Athenians submit to the Medes [Persians] their suffering is guaranteed, for they will be handed over to Hippias. But if the city survives this danger she may well become the foremost city in Greece." Fail-

Troubled about the outcome of his son Theseus's battle with the Minotaur, King Aegeus consults the Delphic priestess.

DIVINING THE WILL OF THE GODS

When the Greek people wanted to know what the future held—for the outcome of a battle, the health of a relative, the success of a voyage—they looked to the deities that figured so prominently in their everyday lives. According to the historian Xenophon, "The gods know all things, and in sacrifices, omens, voices, and dreams they give forewarning to whomever they wish."

To interpret such messages from the gods, the Greeks cast lots, drew meaning from their dreams, or turned to seers who were able to read certain natural signs—such as patterns in the flight of birds, and those that could be found in the sounds of thunder and in the entrails of sacrificed animals. For the most expert opinion, seekers might travel to an oracle, the place where the gods spoke directly to man.

The most famous of these oracles was at Delphi, on Mount Parnassus, northwest of Attica *(left)*. After completing the proper sacrifices, pilgrims submitted questions to the oracle's priestess, who was believed to be directly inspired by Apollo. Falling into a trance, the priestess called out the divine responses, which were then interpreted by an assistant and passed on to the petitioner.

Watched by his family and a slave in barbarian dress, a soldier inspects the entrails of a sacrifice before leaving for war.

ure to fight the Persians, Miltiades went on, would stir up quarrels back in the city and "so shake the will of the Athenians that they will lose their resolve and yield" to the invaders. "Everything depends upon you. If you side with me the land of our fathers will be free and your city will be the first city in Greece."

The general's rhetoric must have worked on Callimachus, for not only did the commander in chief agree to an early attack on the Persians, he also gave Miltiades effective command of the operation.

Now that the battle plan had been decided, it was time to ask for the blessing of the gods. Before leaving the city, Callimachus had visited the shrine of Artemis, goddess of the hunt and "rainer of arrows," to offer the prescribed prayers. But he had done even more: If Artemis gave him victory, he promised to sacrifice annually to her one goat for every Persian slain at Marathon. And now, on the eve of battle, it fell to Miltiades to carry out another ritual: He burned in sacrifice an animal—a goat or perhaps a sheep—then had a seer study the creature's smoking entrails to divine the omens for success. The omens were good. The gods looked favorably on the venture. The hour to fight had come.

Most of the hoplites that had been called to defend democratic Athens against invasion were farmers, typically owners of small, five- to 10-acre plots. But the ranks also included citizens of other occupations, such as wealthy tradesmen and craftsmen, and even sculptors and poets. One of the latter was Aeschylus,

The poet Aeschylus considered his participation in the Battle of Marathon the supreme accomplishment of his life.

who had marched off to battle with his brother and fellow hoplite Cynegeirus. Destined to become the first great playwright of Greek tragedy, Aeschylus noted every detail of the developing war with Persia, storing it all away for future use on the stage.

And as he looked at the men around him on the morning of the battle, the soldier-poet must have wondered about their prospects for victory. For although he would have been stiff and sore after a night spent on the hard ground—probably under the cover of an improvised brushwood hut—he was, at 35, far from being the oldest of the Greek warriors assembled there that day. Gnarled but sturdy old veterans nearing 60 years of age stood next to teenagers whose only experience of war was listening to the stories of their older kin or viewing the armor plundered from the enemy, which adorned the temples of Athens.

Except for these youngest men, the hoplites wore full beards and mustaches, although their hair was cropped short. None of them would have been physically imposing by modern standards: On average, they stood about five feet six inches tall and weighed around 150 pounds, just over twice the weight of the arms and armor that they would wear into battle.

No Greek army, as most Athenians knew, had ever defeated the Persians. And in Aeschylus's imagination, the fearsome reputation of the enemy from across the sea must have grown with every minute that passed that morning. "The enormous army," he would later write of the Persians, "invincible archers and horsemen / terrifying to look upon and formidable in battle, / in the steadfast resolve of their spirit."

As the time for battle approached, Aeschylus would have joined his fellow warriors in a final meal of barley, olives, and onions, washed down with extra rations of wine to help steady the nerves. With the assistance of his slave, he would then don his combat gear. First, over a wool or linen tunic he strapped on his body armor, or cuirass, presumably the so-called bell corselet. This consisted of front diameter and weighing nearly 20 pounds, had a concave wooden core about an inch thick and was covered in highly polished bronze. A hoplite would hold the shield rigidly waist high by running his left arm through a metal band in the middle of the back and then grasping a leather loop near the rim. A lip along the rim allowed him to rest the weight of the shield on his left shoulder when he was not directly engaged. The spear, carried in the right hand, was designed for thrusting, not throwing. It was seven or eight feet long and had a one-inch-thick wooden shaft with a sharp iron spearhead at one end and a bronze butt spike at the other to provide extra killing power. And at his waist Aeschylus would have

"It seemed to them that the Athenians had lost their minds and were bent on destroying themselves."

and back sheets of bronze connected at the shoulder and curving outward like a bell just above the hip. The corselet alone weighed nearly 40 pounds, which explained why some of Aeschylus's comrades may well have been wearing the lighter leather armor that was then coming into fashion.

To protect his shins, calves, and knees, thin bronze greaves were fitted onto Aeschylus's lower legs. These extended down to the ankle-high leather boots, which laced up the front. Onto his head he most likely lowered a five-pound Corinthian helmet, an impressive and beautiful piece of equipment beaten from a single sheet of bronze. The helmet covered everything except the eyes, for which it provided slits, and the mouth. As Aeschylus milled around with the other hoplites waiting for the fighting to begin, he probably pushed this torturous contraption far back on his head, visorlike, in hopes of catching a cool breeze from the Aegean.

Next came Aeschylus's weaponry. The shield, about a yard in carried a short single-edged iron sword for hacking and slashing.

After everyone was armed and armored, the commanding general, Miltiades, arranged his troops in phalanx formation. Ordinarily, the phalanx was rectangular in shape, with the hoplites arrayed many men across and at least eight men deep. But Miltiades knew that he could not maintain that kind of uniform depth against the Persians, whose superior numbers had allowed them to form a line a mile wide. Instead, he elected to stretch the center of his phalanx dangerously thin while providing extra depth on the wings in order to envelop the Persian flanks.

Cautiously, the general moved his men into position in front of the Persian line, just out of range of the enemy archers. By custom, the strongest fighters were found both in the front rank, where they could engage the enemy first, and in the rank at the rear, where they could buck up any fainthearted comrades at the back of the phalanx.

Standing ready for battle under the searing midsummer sun, Aeschylus and many of the bronze-clad warriors of Athens could hear Miltiades shout final instructions: The hoplites would attack on the run, thereby giving the phalanx greater momentum and lessening the period under fire from the Persian archers. It was then, perhaps, that the playwright lowered his helmet over his face, immediately muffling his hearing and restricting his sight to what he could see straight ahead through the narrow eye slits. But still he had no trouble in making out the blast of the trumpetlike *salpinx*. Helmets in front of him began to move forward. The Athenians were advancing on the enemy.

Chanting paeans in praise of their gods, the hoplites lumbered into a jog. Armor chafed their hot, raw skin, and shields and spears jostled together chaotically. Clutching his shield in his left hand, each man instinctively edged to the right, seeking the protection of his neighbor's shield for his vulnerable right side; as it advanced, the entire phalanx veered slightly off to the right.

Across the way, the Persian soldiers were stunned by what they saw. "It seemed to them," wrote Herodotus of the Persians,

"that the Athenians had lost their minds and were bent on destroying themselves." For with every hoplite moving forward at his own speed, the Athenians must have resembled an armed mob rather than the expected disciplined phalanx. What's more, they were charging without the support of cavalry or archers. The surprise seemed to throw off the aim of the Persian archers, and most of their arrows flew over the heads of the attackers; those that hit bounced harmlessly off the heavy Greek shields and armor. The Athenians kept coming.

Looking around, the Persian foot soldiers must have been disconcerted by something else: the absence of their own cavalry. Just what happened to the vaunted Persian horsemen remains a mystery. The most plausible explanation is that they had been sent by ship to make a landing nearer Athens. Whatever the cause, the horsemen were nowhere to be seen as the Athenians approached. This was going to be a battle fought out by infantrymen at close quarters, precisely what the hoplites did best.

By now the front two or three ranks of hoplites were almost upon the enemy, their spears carried in an underhand grip in hopes of scoring below the lightweight Persian body armor. Peering through their eye slits, these lead men were close enough to

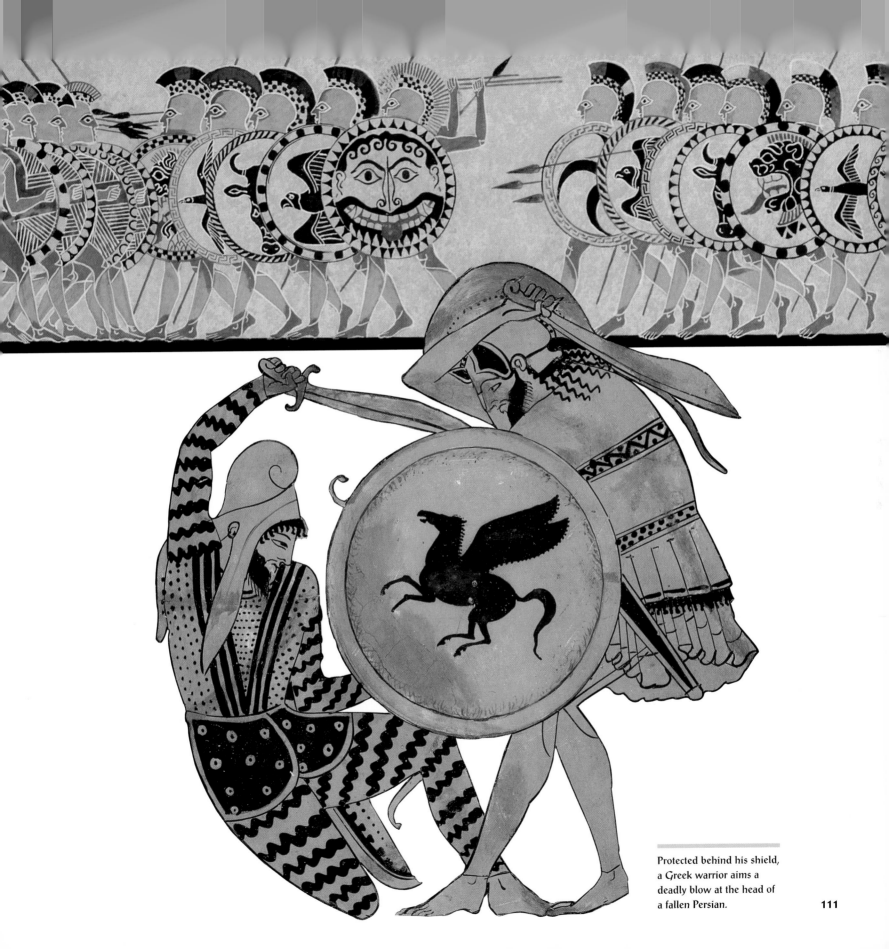

Protected behind his shield, a Greek warrior aims a deadly blow at the head of a fallen Persian.

see the fear on the Persian faces. On the hoplites ran. Then, with a clash of metal and a war cry rising from thousands of throats, the Athenians hurled themselves on the enemy line.

At first the Persians reeled under the impact of the charging phalanx. But then the shallow center of the Athenian ranks foundered against the Persian depth; the middle of the phalanx began to fall back. On the flanks, however, hundreds of personal battles flared. This was what the hoplite-farmers called "threshing it out." There, switching to an overhand grip on their spears, the front ranks thrust down at the vulnerable neck and shoulders of the enemy foot soldiers. And with the pike at the butt end of their spears, hoplites in the other ranks bludgeoned foes who had fallen to the ground. If the spear shaft broke, they stabbed with the remaining length or hacked with their short swords.

As Athenians in the front ranks fell, men behind them stepped forward to fill the breach. But the hoplites in the rear played another, frequently decisive, role. They were essential for what was known as the *othismos*—"the push." Supporting the lip of his shield on his shoulder, each warrior shoved with the shield against the back of the man in front of him. By literally adding the weight of every man to the attack in this way, the othismos could succeed in forcing a breakthrough in the enemy line.

Desperately, the Athenians on both wings strove to maintain their close-ordered ranks and effect just such a breakthrough, while those in the middle tried to hold off the overwhelming Persian numbers that faced them. As each man fought to stand his ground, some undoubtedly battled another, more personal foe—Phobos, the god of fear. For in successful phalanx warfare every hoplite had to be able to count on the man next to him, and none could abandon his assigned place in the line.

Even the hardiest of veterans must have found the close-in combat of this

The example provided by portrayals such as those of a dying warrior *(below)* and a soldier binding the wounds of a comrade *(above)* inspired new Athenian recruits to vow, "I shall not dishonor the sacred arms I bear; I shall never desert my fellow-soldiers."

battle terrifying. In the thick of it was Aeschylus, who would later refer to "the air made insane by the shaking of the spear." Blinded by dust, blood, and sweat, men fought to exhaustion. Delirious under the stress of combat and temperatures that probably reached the 90s, some swore that they saw the armed ghost of Theseus, the early mythological king of Attica, rising from the earth to lead them. Others spoke of a hero named Echetlos who, noted the writer Pausanias, "struck down many of the barbarians with a plowshare, and then could not be found after the battle."

The Persians were indeed falling. An hour or so into the battle, the Athenians succeeded in smashing enemy resistance on both flanks. Then the hoplites on each wing began to wheel and converge on the center, where their outnumbered comrades had been forced back. It was all too much for

the Persians: Overcome by the onslaught of the Greek phalanx, they broke in confusion and fled toward their waiting ships, some two miles away. The Athenians pursued them, cutting down and trampling many. Reaching the shore, they attempted to seize the Persian ships before the invaders could get away. During this action, it was later reported, the polemarch Callimachus suffered what we are told was a hero's death. Herodotus reported anoth-

A lasting monument to the Athenians who fought at Marathon, this 30-foot-high mound marks the resting place of their 192 dead.

er casualty in this melee by the sea: Aeschylus's brother, Cynegeirus, who "had his hand cut off with an ax as he grabbed an ornament on the stern of an enemy ship" and bled to death.

Athenian losses were remarkably low, however. By Herodotus's accounting, only 192 of them died in the battle, compared with the terrible Persian toll of 6,400 men. Hundreds of hoplites must have been wounded, though, and after the Persians rowed their ships out of reach into the bay, the Athenians tended to those who could still be helped. Some had their broken limbs splinted with pieces of spear shaft. Others had wine poured into their wounds to slow the bleeding. And those with large gashes in their flesh had them sutured with needles made of bronze and then covered with dressings of linen or cotton.

But even as these citizen-soldiers bound up the wounds of battle that morning, Miltiades knew that the danger had not passed. For back in Athens the citizens were as yet unaware of the great victory at Marathon; undefended and open to attack,

the city might well surrender to the Persians if the enemy got there first. To prevent this, legend says, Miltiades dispatched a runner to inform the citizenry of the battle's outcome and urge them to hold out. After covering the 26 miles without stopping—a feat commemorated in the modern marathon race—the runner stumbled into Athens. "Rejoice, we conquer!" he supposedly gasped, and then fell dead.

Such heroics, mythical or not, proved unnecessary, however, for the water route of the Persian fleet—southward around the tip of the Attica Peninsula—was nearly three times the land distance to the city. By the time the Persians appeared off the coast near Athens, the hoplites of Miltiades had made it back and now lined the shore, spears at the ready, to meet the invaders. Seeing them, the Persians turned and sailed for home, taking with them the old Athenian tyrant Hippias, who was said to have died on the journey.

It had been a great victory. So many Persians had been slain, in fact, that the Athenian assembly passed a resolution asking Artemis to release the city from its prebattle vow—Callimachus's promise to the goddess to sacrifice annually a goat for every enemy soldier killed. Artemis, tradition has it, graciously accepted the compromise of her petitioners: 500 goats were to be offered up to her every year at the festival that came to be known as Marathon Day.

Their combat finished for that summer, the citizen-soldiers of Athens went back to their homes and their farms, hung their well-used weapons of war over the hearth, and prepared for the September grape harvest. And so they resumed the everyday rhythm of agricultural life, ready for the next call to arms.

But for all those who fought the Persians that fateful day—known ever after as "the men of Marathon"—the battle would remain both a benchmark in their special brand of warfare and a high point in their lives. This was certainly the case for the poet Aeschylus. Although he participated in at least one more major battle and survived to write some 90 plays that placed him at the very pinnacle of the Greek theater, he never forgot his experiences on the plain of Marathon. When he died in 456 BC on a visit to Sicily, the epitaph that he had prepared for his grave bore no mention of his theatrical success. It referred only to that long-ago service as an ordinary hoplite in the Athenian phalanx: "Under this monument lies Aeschylus the Athenian / Euphorion's son, who died in the wheatlands of Gela / The grove of Marathon, with its glories, can speak of his valor in battle / The long-haired Persian remembers and can speak of it too."

After their rebuff at Marathon, the Persians returned to Greece 10 years later—and sacked Athens—only to suffer further defeat at the Battle of Salamis in 480 BC. Unlike Marathon, which was a great victory won by the Athenians, Salamis was fought by men from all over Greece. And unlike Marathon, Salamis was fought at sea.

Winged Victory adds a final touch to this trophy of captured enemy armor and weapons, traditionally erected in thanksgiving on the battlefield.

Despite the magnificent performance of its hoplites in 490 BC, Athens had realized that its defense would require more than a courageous corps of soldier-farmers. In fact, one of the generals who fought at Marathon, Themistokles, advised his fellow citizens to build a navy—and "cleave to the sea." Thus, when a rich lode of silver was found in southern Attica in 483 BC, Themistokles persuaded the Athenians to use the windfall to build a fleet of powerful warships. The mainstay of this new force was the trireme, a warship that carried a 200-man crew and was propelled by oarsmen positioned on three levels. These triremes gradually supplanted the hoplite as the backbone of Athenian military might; with them, the city-state was able to achieve maritime supremacy in the eastern Mediterranean and maintain it for much of the following century and a half.

But the operation of a navy was an expensive undertaking. While the newly mined

lodoros—who was also a banker—had volunteered for appointment to the trierarchy.

As trierarch, Apollodoros was expected to muster the crew for one warship, who would be paid and fed by the state. He was also expected to serve as captain of the vessel for 12 months and to pay for any damage that it sustained during his term of office. But Apollodoros was a man of expensive tastes and inordinate pride. Ordered into active service in 362 BC, he was determined to achieve something of a deluxe trierarchy: He intended to hire the most skilled crew and operate the best-equipped trireme in the entire Athenian navy.

For a start, Apollodoros chose not to rely on the ropes, ladders, masts, and other gear routinely supplied by the government. "I furnished the ship with equipment wholly my own," he said later, "taking nothing from the public stores, and I made everything as beautiful

"I made everything as beautiful and magnificent as possible, outdoing all the other trierarchs."

silver could finance construction of a fleet that eventually comprised more than 300 triremes, it could not maintain the costly fleet for very long. To do that, Athens had to rely on its wealthiest citizens, allowing them to serve one-year terms as so-called trierarchs, in partial fulfillment of their tax obligations. One man who opted for such service was a banker named Apollodoros.

Apollodoros came from an extraordinary family. His father, Pasion, had been a slave employed as an accountant in his master's bank. But through hard work, Pasion had won his freedom, become a banker himself—and was reputed to be the richest man in Athens. Pasion had also won full citizenship for his family from the Athenian assembly, and in gratitude, his son Apol-

and magnificent as possible, outdoing all the other trierarchs."

Finding sailors to man the ship was more difficult than outfitting it, however. Generally, crewmembers were raised from among the thetes. But only a few thetes actually reported for duty with Apollodoros—"and these incompetent," he complained. Dismissing them, he borrowed money and began looking for a freelance crew.

The task was considerable. For in addition to rowers—he needed 170 of them—Apollodoros had to find deck hands, a contingent of 10 hoplites to serve as marines, four archers, a purser, a bow officer to keep watch, and a boatswain to oversee the rowers. Most important, he required a good helmsman, who, in addition to taking charge of the navigation, would serve as the trierarch's technical adviser, his most experienced officer, and his second-in-command.

To get such a crew, Apollodoros had to depart from the usual hiring procedures. Normally sailors were paid no more than a drachma a day, and half of that was usually held back until the completion of the tour of duty. The wealthy banker felt no obligation to limit himself to the going rates, however; touring the waterfront at Piraeus, Athens's bustling port, he sought out only the most experienced seamen—namely, the thetes, resident aliens, and foreign mercenaries who had learned their trade in the merchant marine. "I was the first to man my ship," he bragged, "hiring sailors of the best possible quality by giving large bounties and payments in advance."

The departure of Apollodoros's crew was likely a grand occasion. Accompanied by crowds of loved ones and well-wishers, the new recruits would have marched out of Athens at dawn, following the walls that formed a protective corridor between the city and Piraeus, five miles to the southwest. Apollodoros may well have traveled with his crewmen. Extravagant, showy—and eager to prove himself worthy of citizenship—the new trierarch must have been bursting with pride as he made his way to Piraeus. His heart would have leaped when he saw the long, sleek triremes bobbing at the wharves in the port's natural harbors. Then he would have spotted his own ship, newly outfitted and ready to embark. Like the others, it was about 150 feet long and 20 feet wide, fashioned from a combination of imported woods —oak, fir, pine, or cedar. A sturdy bronze ram jutted forward menacingly from its keel.

As he stepped aboard—the crowds cheering—Apollodoros surely felt a sense of importance he had never before experienced. He may well have reflected on his assigned mission of escorting back to Athens merchant ships carrying vital grain from the Black Sea; on his family's humble origins and their struggle to gain acceptance within Athenian society; on the hardships that his wife and young children might face while he was gone; on the thrill that he felt when he was first appointed trierarch.

The sound of a trumpet would have brought Apollodoros back to the present. For this was the signal for prayers to be offered up for a safe and successful voyage. Wine was poured as a libation, and everyone joined in singing praises to the gods. Then the oars flashed and the ships pulled away. At first, they moved in line astern but then fanned out, racing to see which would be the first to pass the island of Aegina, 10 or so miles offshore, in full view of the shorebound spectators.

And so began the first of many missions that Apollodoros performed during his trierarchy. During these voyages his trireme would have hugged the shoreline whenever possible. For while his ship was sturdy, it was comparatively light and was difficult to handle in a strong wind. And even though the trireme was equipped with two masts, the deck hands would have hoisted the papyrus or white flax sails only in the most favorable winds and at times when speed was not a primary consideration. The trireme relied mainly on oar power, which was faster, propelling the vessel at an average speed of up to eight knots in normal circumstances, or about 9.2 miles per hour. In combat, with their adrenaline flowing, the rowers could generate quick bursts of speed up to 13 knots for a period of 10 to 20 minutes.

The 170 human sources of this power were packed tightly belowdecks on wooden benches on three superimposed levels. Each man had his own personal leather cushion; tallow on the cushion bottom allowed it to slide back and forth with the oarsman as he alternately straightened his legs and brought his body forward to help drive the trireme forward. It was hot, monotonous, backbreaking work, and sometimes it had to be endured—with little respite—for as many as 17 hours a day.

In times of emergency, the oarsmen might consume their meals aboard the ship, downing a kind of combat ration of bar-

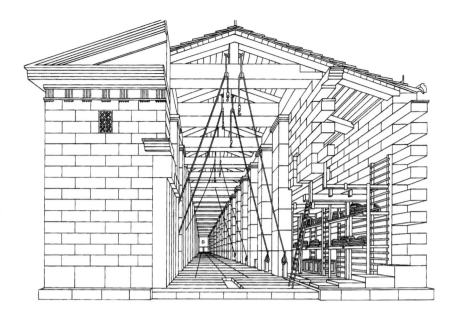

ley bread mixed with wine and olive oil while rowing. They would take turns rowing and sleeping until the crisis passed. The usual practice, however, was to go ashore for the midday meal and then again at night to eat and bivouac. To stay light and agile for maneuvering, triremes typically carried only a few days' provisions, mostly barley, dried fish, cheese, onions, garlic, and olives. Supply ships or commercial vessels operated by tradesmen sometimes accompanied long expeditions. Otherwise, sailors were given a daily allowance and purchased food ashore from local inhabitants.

During a voyage, trireme crews drilled constantly, holding races and performing mock battles in order to sharpen their power, speed, and agility. Over the years these drills changed as the techniques of naval warfare themselves changed. In the early days of the Athenian navy, for example, the trireme was thought of mainly as a moving platform: From its deck, archers and javelin

Constructed in accordance with archaeological remains found at Piraeus, the modern trireme *Olympias (below)* cuts through the water at speeds of up to 15 miles per hour. When not in use, Greek triremes and their gear hung in sheds like the one above to preserve their wooden hulls, cloth sails, and ropes.

throwers could unleash their missiles, and its contingent of heavily armored marine hoplites could slug it out with their opposite numbers on the enemy ship as if in an infantry engagement on land. But soon tacticians realized that the trireme itself could become a potent offensive weapon—especially when armed with a 400-pound bronze-and-wood ram and a trio of sharp blades jutting from the keel at the bow.

One favorite set of maneuvers that Apollodoros would have practiced called for his ship to circle the enemy or to dart through his line—and then swing around to ram him in the stern or other vulnerable spot. Such tactics required superb steering by the Athenian helmsman, who had to turn his ship in the same direction as his target just before impact to prevent his ram from being ripped loose.

Just what use Apollodoros and his men made of their training and their tactical maneuvers in actual battle is not part of the historical record. But we do know that his trireme proved to be the fastest in the fleet and that one of the navy's generals even selected it as his flagship.

Indeed, Apollodoros seems to have performed the job of trierarch so zealously that he had to serve an additional five months beyond his scheduled year of duty. His successor, a man named Polycles, blamed his unreadiness on Apollodoros, claiming that the banker had made the trierarchy too expensive. He accused Apollodoros of "madness and extravagance" and of corrupting the crew with "large sums of money." Because of this, Polycles told Apollodoros, "you have been the teacher of bad practices in the navy."

By now Apollodoros's enthusiasm to serve had turned to resentment. But he knew that there was recourse for a wealthy citizen of democratic Athens—access to the courts—and Apollodoros intended to exercise this option with the same zest with which he had begun his naval service. He brought suit against Polycles for the costs incurred in the extra five months in service. He sued his old general, alleging that he had accepted an illegal loan from Polycles to overlook the delay in doing his duty. And he went on to sue other prominent figures in Athenian society.

Some changes in the trierarchy system were already under way that would ease the required burden on the wealthy, however. One reform allowed two citizens to share the responsibility, with each spending six months as ship commander. And soon after Apollodoros's financial ordeal, further alterations in the law distributed the load by providing for each trierarchy to be handled by a syndicate made up of a number of citizens.

But from what we know of him, we can imagine that Apollodoros's pride and flair for the extravagant would never have allowed him to shoulder less than the full burden of a trierarchy. In fact, these attributes and his penchant for litigation quickly consumed the fortune left him by his father. By age 45 Apollodoros, the spendthrift banker, was a bankrupt former ship captain, left with little more than the memories of those exhilarating—and expensive—days at sea.

The annals of the Athenian navy featured another commander with a powerful need to prove himself. This young man was the offspring of even more notable parentage than Apollodoros, for if the latter was the son of the richest man in Athens, then Pericles, son of Pericles, was (as his name implies) the son of the most powerful—none other than the great leader and general himself. But in his youth, the younger Pericles had carried the taint of illegitimacy as the son of Aspasia, the leader's common-law wife; "Aspasia's bastard," theatrical comedians had called him. And because Aspasia was foreign born, he was ineligible for citizenship, thanks to the citizenship law put forth by his own father that required both parents to be native-born Athenians.

This stigma was lifted only after the elder Pericles had won from the assembly an exception to the law; his son was then awarded citizenship and the right to carry on the illustrious family name. And when the 33-year-old Pericles was elected gen-

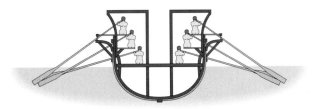

As shown in the diagram above, three banks of trireme rowers pulled together as a team, with the lower-level rowers, the *zugites* and the *thalamites*, following the strokes of the top-level *thranites*, the only group able to see their oars enter the water. Thranites, seen straining in unison in the fifth-century bas-relief below, balanced their oars on an outrigger, a support that extended beyond the ship's side to give greater leverage.

eral in 407 BC, he determined to follow the advice laid down by his father in the famous funeral oration honoring the Athenian dead: "These take as your model, and judging happiness to be the fruit of freedom and freedom of courage, never decline the dangers of war."

The dangers of war had become all too familiar to the people of Athens by the time of the younger Pericles' generalship. For by then Athens had been fighting Sparta—its old ally in the struggle against Persia—for a quarter of a century. At stake in this fratricidal war was the position of dominance in Greece.

Firmly established as a sea power ever since the defeat of the Persians at Salamis in 480 BC, Athens had begun to expand its influence among its neighbors, turning them into allies and exporting to them its democracy. This it did at the expense of Sparta, the great warrior state ruled by a privileged oligarchy. As a result, the other city-states were drawn into two camps: The islands of the Aegean and the coastal cities of Asia Minor sided with Athens, while the states of southern Greece formed an alliance with Sparta. War became inevitable, and these southern states located in the Peloponnesos gave the conflict its name: the Peloponnesian War.

For most of the war, which pitted the naval strength of Athens against Spartan superiority in land warfare, the two sides were at a stalemate, neither one able to deliver the decisive blow. So it was that by the last decade of the fifth century BC, the Athenian populace had grown discouraged by the length and cost of the conflict. Moreover, during the course of the war the Spartans had developed their own fleet and were beginning to assert themselves on the seas, too. In the year 406, news of a reversal in the eastern Aegean stunned Athens. That summer a Spartan commander named Callicratidas had caught the Athenian fleet at the entrance to the harbor of Mytilene on the island of Lesbos, just off the coast of Asia Minor. His armada sank 30 Athenian ships and bottled up the remaining 40 by blockading the harbor while he sent infantry to cut off all supply routes by land. One Athenian vessel managed to slip through the blockade and race home with the news.

The people of Athens responded immediately to the crisis: A fleet of about 150 Athenian and allied triremes was scraped together from existing vessels, from ships under construction, and from ships undergoing repair. To man the fleet, improvised crews were quickly recruited, drawing men from all classes of society, including hoplites and high-born cavalrymen as well as foreigners and slaves (the latter now induced to fight by promises of citizenship and freedom, respectively). Under the command of young Pericles and seven other generals, the new fleet put to sea within a month.

Sailing eastward, the Athenian armada soon caught up with Callicratidas in the channel between Lesbos and the mainland of Asia Minor. There, just west of the Arginoussai Islands, the opposing fleets squared off. On this particular summer morning, the usual tactical situation was reversed: Although the Athenians outnumbered the Spartans by at least 30 ships, both sides knew that the hastily assembled Athenian fleet and crews were no match for those of the Spartans in terms of speed or skill.

The disparity between the two sides was reflected in their formations. Callicratidas deployed the squadrons of his fleet so that each formed a single file, ready to break through the enemy line and then wheel around to ram. This was a tactic normally employed by the Athenians; now the Spartan commander intended to beat his adversaries at their own game. By contrast, Pericles and his fellow generals arranged their squadrons—each 10 to 15 ships strong—in a more defensive alignment, one aimed at preventing a Spartan breakthrough in the Athenian line or an envelopment around its flanks. That line was a long one, extending for about 4,000 yards, and on each flank the generals had concentrated particular strength, deploying triremes there 10 deep. On the very left of the line Pericles took up his position.

As he awaited the approach of the enemy, Pericles must have pondered his chances of success that day. He was well aware that by this stage of the war the once landbound Spartans had become capable sailors. And he knew, too, the strength of the fleet that opposed him. But this was not all that worried him. Like all Greeks, young Pericles put a lot of stock in the ability of the priests who accompanied the fleet to foretell the future. And the predictions made earlier that morning were at best mixed. On the one hand they declared that the Athenians would, indeed, achieve a great victory, but on

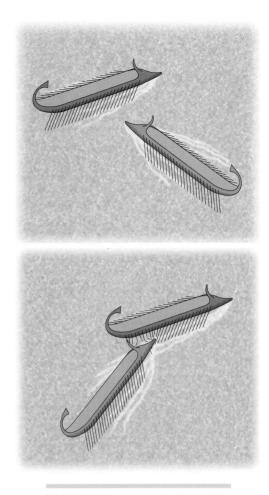

THE TRIREME AS WEAPON

The Athenians were expert at using their light, fast warships to ram enemy galleys amidships *(top)*, a vessel's weakest point. But the trireme crew had to be ready to abruptly reverse direction so that the enemy had no time to grapple and board the attacking ship.

Another of their tactics was to row close enough to shear off an enemy's oars on one side, a tricky move that could cripple an opponent. Well-drilled Athenian rowers skillfully executed such moves because they spent so much time at sea protecting their naval empire; other city-states—who maintained fleets only during times of war—were less adept.

THE MAKING OF A SPARTAN

Compared with the spirited Athenians, the people of the city-state of Sparta seemed to possess an overabundance of self-denial, loyalty, courage, and discipline. These attributes, however, served to make them the undisputed land power in Greece in the fifth century BC. Such military prowess was not surprising for a society that saw its primary role as that of producing warriors. While a large, hostile population of state-owned serfs known as helots tilled the land, Spartan citizens were free to concentrate on preparing for war.

Such preparations began at an early age—from birth, in fact, when a committee of elders ordered that weak infants be left to die on the slopes of a nearby mountain. At seven, boys went to live in army barracks and began strenuous endurance training. During their teenage years, the boys, deprived of adequate food and clothing, underwent two particularly difficult

Cloaked and helmeted Spartan warriors
like this one carefully dressed their long
hair before going into battle.

Protected by mountains, Sparta's fertile plain provided an isolated environment for the state's distinct culture.

trials. One required them to run a gauntlet to snatch as many cheeses as they could from the steps of an altar to Artemis. Another sent them out alone into the countryside to live by their wits and to kill helots. At 20, males became full citizens, although they continued to live communally until the age of 30. Even when a young man married, he still slept and ate with his comrades, secretly rendezvousing with his wife at night.

Spartan training produced unswerving patriotism. The Spartan warrior was prepared, in the words of one poet, to "hold his shield fast / making his own life his enemy, and the black spirits / of Death as dear to him as the rays of the sun." But Sparta was unable to maintain its influence. Defeated in 371 BC by a coalition of Greek states, the once dominant power retreated into isolationism, its tradition of military invincibility gone forever.

SPARTAN WOMEN

Just as Spartan males were raised to become warriors, so the women of Sparta were trained for their primary task: giving birth to warriors. Encouraged to be strong and healthy, girls participated in athletic competitions, running footraces in off-the-shoulder chitons like that worn by the bronze figure above.

Spartan girls also were taught music, dance, and poetry, along with household management and child rearing, to become the best mothers they could be. Unquestioning in the performance of their duty, Spartan mothers did not give in to sentiment even when faced with a child's death. "I bore him so that he might die for Sparta," one woman said of her son, "and that is what has happened, as I wished."

123

the other they foretold that seven of the eight generals present would lose their lives.

Spartan priests had been making their own forecasts that morning—and they had predicted a dire fate for their own leader. In fact, so worried had the Spartans become that the helmsman of Callicratidas's flagship had even urged him to retire without giving battle. But Callicratidas would have none of it; he took up his position

tore off one great part from another," wrote Diodorus. But in so doing, the ram of Callicratidas's own vessel had become stuck in the Athenian ship, and his oarsmen were unable to pull clear of it. Pericles was not about to let the enemy commander out of his clutches, even if it meant becoming one of the seven Athenian generals supposedly destined for death. He threw grappling irons into the Spartan ship and forced it in close so that the two vessels rode side by side. The op-

"If I die, Sparta will go on just the same."

on the fleet's right wing, the traditional post for the commander of the fleet—and the one that faced Pericles in the Athenian line. "If I die, Sparta will go on just the same," Callicratidas declared with characteristic Spartan courage and fatalism. "What is disgraceful is to run away."

Neither side was about to run away. With the sailors of Athens and Sparta now ready, trumpet calls rent the air, and crews on both sides sent up a great cheer. Minutes later some 270 triremes were under way, carrying over 50,000 men into battle. "Plying their oars with great heat and earnestness," wrote the historian Diodorus Siculus, "every one strove who should be the first in making onset."

Leading the charge was Callicratidas, whose squadron quickly sank several Athenian ships. "Others he disabled," recorded Diodorus, "striking them through with the beaks of his ships, and others he made useless for fight by brushing off their oars." If the Spartan leader were going to die as predicted, the historian noted, he "endeavored to make his death honorable and glorious."

Callicratidas was on a collision course with Pericles. "At length he struck the ship of Pericles with such violence that he

posing marines must have gone at it hand to hand in true hoplite fashion, their spears and swords flashing in the midday sun while shipwrecked survivors thrashed around them in the choppy waters of the Aegean.

Among the casualties was the Spartan commander. According to Diodorus, "Callicratidas, after he had behaved himself with great gallantry a long time and received many wounds in all parts of his body, at length wearied out, fell down dead." In the words of another chronicler, Xenophon, the Spartan "fell overboard and disappeared in the water."

Leaderless, the Spartan right wing crumbled and fled in the face of a bold counterattack led by Pericles and three other Athenian generals. The Spartan left wing soon followed. "The greatest sea fight that was ever fought by Greek against Greek"— as Diodorus described it—was over.

It had, indeed, been a bloody affair. The Athenians lost 13 ships and 12 more were disabled. But the enemy losses were worse: Some 70 Spartan vessels sank and many thousands of sailors died. Pericles and the other generals could rejoice in the predicted triumph and, in the face of the prophecy, their own happy survival.

The rejoicing was short lived, however, for soon the generals were agonizing over what to do next. Hundreds of their comrades clung desperately to the wreckage of lost and disabled ships in hopes of rescue. Among them floated the bodies of the dead who, by tradition, had to be retrieved for proper burial. At the same time, an untouched portion of the Spartan fleet—some 50 vessels—remained on the blockade of Mytilene harbor, ripe for attack. After debating at length which task to carry out, the gen-

erals compromised: 75 ships would sail to Mytilene to lift the siege, while 47 others, under the command of two trierarchs, Theramenes and Thrasybulus, would rescue the survivors of Arginoussai. By the time the generals had reached this decision, however, a gale had sprung up—and they were able neither to attack Mytilene nor to pick up the survivors and the dead.

When news of the battle reached Athens, the citizens at first rejoiced at another great naval victory. But as more details be-

With their spears at the ready, two soldiers play a board game during a lull in the fighting.

came available about exactly what had happened in the eastern Aegean, the people's celebrations turned to horror at the scale of the losses. The public mood worsened when the trierarchs Theramenes and Thrasybulus returned to the city and helped stir up a popular outcry against the generals: The eight were recalled to Athens for trial before the ekklesia.

As he journeyed back across the sea to face his accusers, Pericles must have replayed in his mind the final events of the Battle of Arginoussai—and rehearsed the defense that he would use in the assembly. Some of the generals had wanted to blame the failure of the rescue mission on the two trierarchs entrusted with the assignment. But Pericles had helped talk them out of it: The violence of the storm, he insisted, was the only reason why the survivors had not been picked up. And while two of the eight generals had opted to go into exile rather than stand trial in Athens, Pericles was determined to present his case to the people.

Still, Pericles surely considered the trial with some trepidation. When he arrived at Athens and was escorted to one of the city's jails, he would have recalled that his own father had been put through what the historian Thucydides called "the usual fickleness of the multitude." The elder Pericles had been censured, fined, and stripped of his rank as general by the assembly because of popular discontent about the war (although he was elected general again soon thereafter). If this could happen to the so-called first citizen of Athens, then anything was possible now, given the war weariness of the city. Was it possible, he must have wondered to himself, that the two generals who had not returned with the others had been right to flee after all?

Such thoughts no doubt weighed heavily on Pericles' mind as he rose to address the Athenian assembly. We do not know

how good a speaker young Pericles was; he probably could not match the flair of his father. But we do know that each of the six generals was permitted to speak in his own defense (although for less time than that allowed by the law). Pericles and the others made clear that they could have blamed their accusers, Theramenes and Thrasybulus, but that the weather was the true cause of the postbattle disaster. Sentiment in the assembly seemed to be shifting their way. But evening was upon them, and it soon became too dark to count the show of hands needed for a verdict. The assembly decided to adjourn for the day.

The adjournment proved tragic for the accused. For in the boule, the council that shaped the agenda of the larger assembly, a member bribed by Theramenes proposed that the generals be tried collectively rather than individually; and if found guilty, he maintained, they should all be punished with death.

The corrupt councilmember made his arguments persuasively. He emphasized not only the shipwrecked men who might have been saved but also the dead whose bodies were not recovered; such Athenian warriors, he reasoned, were surely deserving

BURYING THE DEAD

In Athens a funeral was a three-part ritual. First, female relatives laid out the corpse at home; below, the women surround the bier, lamenting and tearing at their grief-shorn hair, while men raise their arms in a gesture of farewell to the deceased. Next came the procession to the graveyard, and finally the interment of the remains.

Athenians slain in battle were honored with a civic ceremony. With the community in attendance, the dead were carried to a special military cemetery outside the city, where an orator would deliver a eulogy known as the *epitaphios logos.* The names of the interred were engraved on a funeral stele, a marble slab like the one at right, which shows a man sitting at the prow of his ship with his helmet and shield resting beside him.

of funeral rites befitting heroes of the battlefield. Theramenes exploited these concerns fully. According to Xenophon, the trierarch and his supporters packed the next meeting of the assembly with phony mourners: "Theramenes and his party made arrangement by which a number of people, dressed in black and with hair close-shaven, should attend the assembly, pretending to be kinsmen of those who had been lost after the battle."

Theramenes' machinations had the desired effect in the assembly. But in the generals' defense an eloquent advocate stood up to speak. Euryptolemus, a cousin of young Pericles, insisted that the proposal to try the generals together was unconstitutional. This only incensed the citizens, however, some of whom shouted back that *they* were sovereign and could do as they pleased. Euryptolemus then appealed to their respect for the law. "You are Athenians, and Atheni-

icles and the other five generals who had returned to Athens were quickly put to death, in a manner left unrecorded by the historians. The "fickleness of the multitude" had asserted itself once more, and most of the Athenian seers' prophecies before the Battle of Arginoussai had been fulfilled.

The unfortunate generals had been subject to the worst excesses of the all-powerful assembly. "Soon afterwards," wrote Xenophon, "the Athenians regretted what they had done and voted that complaints should be lodged against those who had deceived the people." But with the Spartan victory in 405 BC and Athens's subsequent surrender in 404, the flame of Athenian democracy would begin to flicker. It would dim further with the arrival of the Macedonians under Philip and his son, Alexander the Great, and then finally burn out in 322 BC—a year after Alexander's death—when a

"You are Athenians, and Athenians do not act like this."

ans do not act like this," he told them. "The laws are your own creation, and it is the laws, above all, which have made you great."

In ruling on procedural questions, the only member of the presiding council who refused to flout the law was the 64-year-old philosopher Socrates, who seven years later would find himself condemned by the people. Desperately, Euryptolemus made a final plea to give each defendant a separate trial and more time to speak. "Men of Athens," he pleaded, "you have won a great and fortunate victory. Do not act as though you were smarting under the ignominy of defeat."

It was futile. The men of Athens were fed up with the war—and even with victory when they deemed the cost too great. In a fit of blood lust, they voted to convict all eight defendants. Per-

large force of Athenian ships went down to defeat at the hands of a more powerful Macedonian fleet.

That the fire of this great experiment in democracy would continue to burn in the human heart had been foreseen a century earlier, however, in the Funeral Oration of the elder Pericles. Ever hopeful, he was convinced that his Athens would be long remembered for what it had briefly been. The great statesman said as much when he reminded his fellow Athenians, "The admiration of the present and succeeding ages will be ours, since we have not left our power without witness. We have forced every sea and land to be the highway of our daring, and everywhere, whether for evil or good, have left imperishable monuments behind us."

A SHADOW FALLS

In 367 BC, a 15-year-old boy named Philip arrived in the city of Thebes from the state of Macedonia. Perhaps some seer reading entrails that day drew back in alarm, but there was no public outcry, no warning that a shadow had just fallen over the future of Greek democracy.

Macedonia, located at the northern border of the Greek world, had recently negotiated an alliance with Thebes—now the strongest military power among the city-states—and as a guarantee of good faith had sent its prince, Philip, to live in the city. Once there, he began studying the structure and tactics of the Theban army, including the fabled Sacred Band, an elite infantry corps. The workings of Greek democracy also caught his attention since Thebes, like Athens, was a democratic city-state. A true son of Macedonia, a land ruled by powerful local chieftains controlled by a king, he probably was not impressed. The constant debate and turnover of power that a democracy required could prove to be fatal weaknesses.

Philip returned to Macedonia in 364 BC and four years later ascended its throne. The new king used what he had learned in Thebes to build one of the world's greatest armies—a force that would be turned against Greek autonomy. In 356 BC, his wife bore him a son. He too would threaten the Greeks, but he would also march against their ancient enemy Persia, earn an empire, and acquire a fitting title—Alexander the Great *(right)*.

Philip, king of Macedonia *(right)*, married at least seven women, the third being a princess from Epirus named Olympias *(above)*, who gave birth to Alexander. Politically ambitious and determined, Olympias, according to rumors, plotted Philip's assassination after his fifth wife, a native Macedonian named Cleopatra, bore him a son—a potential rival to Alexander.

PHILIP AND ALEXANDER AT THE GATES OF ATHENS

"He will not stop, unless some one oppose him," the statesman Demosthenes warned fellow Athenians in 351 BC. "By the gods I believe that Philip is intoxicated with the magnitude of his exploits." He was not the only worried Greek. Since becoming Macedonia's king, Philip had strengthened his border territories, taken control of Thessaly, and made inroads into Thrace.

Not long after Demosthenes' warning, Philip besieged Olynthus on the Chalkidike Peninsula, which bordered Macedonia. Demosthenes urged the Athenian assembly to send defensive troops to Olynthus, thereby carrying the fight to Philip rather than waiting for his army to march on Athens. The Athenians debated too long, however, and Olynthus fell. Despite signing a treaty with Macedonia in 346, Athens had no illusions about Philip's ultimate aim: That same year he took Thermopylae, leaving him in control of the main route into Attica.

In Macedonia, Philip waged another campaign: educating an unruly Alexander. Around 343 BC, the king hired Aristotle to teach the boy. The philosopher surely had his hands full, but he helped shape the prince's interests in natural sciences and literature, and the future king undoubtedly appreciated Aristotle's *Politics*. While praising democracy's virtues, the work justifies monarchy when *arete*, or personal achievement, demands it: "when the arete of the king or of his family is so preeminent that it outclasses the arete of all the citizens put together."

In 340 BC Philip attacked Byzantium, and, alarmed that its vital grain supplies would be imperiled, Athens aided the Byzantines. When the king seized control of an Athenian grain fleet, Athens declared war. Philip marched into Greece in 338, and the Thebans and the Athenians, recently allied, met his troops near Chaironeia. The Macedonians routed the Greeks, although the Sacred Band of Thebes fought until the bitter end, cut down almost to a man by Philip's cavalry—led by the 18-year-old Alexander.

Little now blocked the way from Chaironeia to Athens; the city girded itself for the worst. But Philip offered generous terms: If it abandoned most territorial claims, disbanded its maritime league, and joined in an alliance with Macedonia, the city could preserve its internal democracy. Athens agreed. Philip then worked his diplomatic charms to convene a Panhellenic conference at Corinth, at which he compelled the Greek states to form a Hellenic league and name him its commander. Now he would be able to keep the Greeks in check while drawing manpower and resources from them.

Son of a Macedonian court physician, Aristotle (above) left his homeland to study at Plato's Academy in Athens, returning years later to tutor Alexander.

CONQUEST AND LEGACY

Early in 336 BC, news of great import reached Athens: Philip had fallen to an assassin's blade. Many in the Greek city-states rejoiced, and the Athenian assembly voted a gold crown to the murderer. Alexander, barely 20, quickly assumed his father's mantle and marched south to subdue the Greeks. The appearance of his army in full battle array before Thebes convinced both it and Athens to acknowledge his leadership. But the following year Thebes challenged him again: Alexander razed the city and enslaved its people. Fear gripped the other city-states, and much of the public opposition to his authority collapsed.

Having secured Greece, Alexander gathered an army of Macedonians, Greeks, Thessalians, and Thracians and marched into Persia. He won stunning victories against the Persian king Darius at the river Granicus and at Issus *(opposite)*. From there he headed south into Egypt, where he was proclaimed pharaoh. Marching eastward once again he defeated Darius decisively at Gaugamela and marched unopposed to Babylon. He continued into India, where he defeated the Indian king Porus at the river Hydaspes. After 11 years of fighting, his exhausted army refused to go any farther, and he had to turn homeward.

In Babylon Alexander fell victim to a fever and died in 323, not yet 33 years old.

Hearing the news, Athens again sought to throw off its Macedonian chains, joining the states of northern Greece in revolt. Macedonia's new ruler, Antipater, brutally crushed the rebellion and significantly curtailed the Athenian system of government.

Though democracy in Greece had been damaged by the Macedonians, Greek culture flourished, kept alive by the conquerors themselves. Alexander and his army, which contained not only Greek soldiers but also Greek naturalists and surveyors, and Alexander's successors spread Greek thought, literature, and architecture across the empire. Buried within that rich legacy was the idea of democracy.

Over 11 years, Alexander and his army marched some 8,000 miles as shown on the map, which traces their route from Macedonia through Persia, Egypt, India, and back. Along the way he founded more than a dozen cities named Alexandria, as well as one, Bucephala *(near left)*, named after his favorite horse. Alexander's empire spanned three continents, but without his leadership it fell apart. The Indian conquests reverted to their original rulers; the rest were divided among his generals.

In this portrait, Alexander wears the hide of the Nemean lion slain by Herakles, an allusion to the claim that Alexander was the mythical hero's descendant.

The Persian king Darius retreats in his chariot before the onslaught of Alexander and his army *(above, left)* in a mosaic of the Battle of Issus. Alexander rode into most of his battles on his horse Bucephalas *(right)*, who received a state funeral at his death.

GLOSSARY

Acropolis: "upper city"; a hilltop citadel, a common feature of ancient Greek cities; it offered an elevated site for religious observances and refuge from enemies. The best-known acropolis is that of Athens.

Agora: "assembly"; the open space that served as the civic center and marketplace of ancient Greek cities; it was typically bordered by colonnaded administrative buildings and temples, as at Athens.

Amphora: a two-handled jar used for the storage and transport of wine, oil, dried fish, and other commodities; decorative versions were used as decanters or prizes in games. Many amphorae were stamped before firing, often with a date or the potter's name.

Andron: meaning "men's room"; the most elaborate room in a Greek house, designed for entertaining and dining on couches. It was generally square shaped with a surfaced floor and decorated walls.

Aphrodite: the goddess of love, beauty, and sex; the protectress of prostitutes and sailors; wife of Hephaistos. Her image frequently adorned the handles and covers of women's hand mirrors.

Apollo: son of Zeus, god of music, healing, poetry, and prophecy, epitomizing Greek ideals of male beauty, culture, and moral virtue. Like his twin sister, Artemis, he was frequently portrayed as an archer.

Ares: god of war, lover of Aphrodite. Although regarded as an Olympian god, he did not have a prominent role in myth or religious practice. He was typically represented more as a troublemaker than as a heroic figure.

Aristocracy: meaning "power of the best"; an early form of government in ancient Greece in which the hereditary, landowning nobility was in charge of the state. The group's power waned in much of Greece after the eighth century BC as the middle-class hoplites replaced the aristocratic knights as the most effective fighting force and as commercial development brought wealth to new families.

Artemis: the virgin goddess of the hunt and of wildlife, often shown with a deer or a bow and arrow. She was Zeus's daughter and Apollo's twin sister. Artemis was regarded as the protectress of women giving birth or making the transition from maiden to matron.

Asia Minor: the western Asian peninsula comprising most of modern-day Turkey, known to the Greeks as Anatolia; Greeks settled along its Mediterranean and Black Sea coastlines and throughout nearby islands.

Asklepios: god of medicine, with sanctuaries throughout the Greek world. Although his more fully divine father, Apollo, was also a god of healing, Asklepios was believed to take a greater interest in an individual's well-being. The sacred snake was his primary symbol; whenever a new healing shrine was established by his followers, it was sent a snake from his cult's main temple at Epidaurus.

Athena: virgin goddess of war and crafts, daughter of Zeus, and patron goddess of Athens. She was credited with inventing the aulos *(see below)* and introducing the olive tree; she is normally depicted in armor with a sword and shield.

Attica: a 1,000-square-mile promontory in southeast central Greece that formed the territory of the Athenian city-state; its rugged terrain yielded high-quality marble and potter's clay as well as silver and lead.

Aulos: a wind instrument made of ivory, wood, or bone with finger holes and a double or single reed in the mouthpiece. A musician normally played a pair of pipes, kept in place by a band worn around the head and cheeks. Although popular, the aulos was not considered as noble an instrument as the lyre.

Boule: term for the council of a Greek city-state; sometimes also applied to councils of federated or allied city-states. In fifth-century-BC Athens, the 500-member democratic boule met daily (except for holidays and days of ill omen) to carry out such tasks as preparing the agenda for meetings of the *ekklesia,* auditing state finances, and supervising boards.

Bouleuterion: common name for the meeting place of the council of a Greek city-state; typically a square or rectangular building housing an auditorium with tiered seating.

Cella: The principal room of a Greek temple, where the cult statue of the god was located and, frequently, the temple's treasure was kept. The room was typically rectangular in shape with a single doorway facing east.

Classical Age: term referring to the period of Greek history that begins with the defeat of the Persian invaders in 480-479 BC and ends with Alexander the Great's accession in 336 BC or with his death in 323 BC; the high point of ancient Greek and, specifically, Athenian political power and culture.

Colonies: overseas settlements established on islands or along coastlines near the city-states of Greece, on islands in the Aegean, and in Asia Minor, generally to relieve domestic social and economic pressures or to promote trade. The main era of colonization lasted from 750 BC to 550 BC and saw the foundation of important settlements in Sicily, southern Italy and France, and the Black Sea area. Corinth and Miletus were among the most active colonizers.

Colonnaded: having a continuous row of columns.

Corinth: a leading city of ancient Greece famous for its architecture, pottery, and shipbuilding; its location near the isthmus joining the Peloponnesos to central Greece and its access to the Aegean and Ionian Seas gave it a prominent role in communications, trade, and naval affairs. The city built a special—and highly profitable—toll road across the isthmus to allow merchant ships to be dragged between the two seas, thereby avoiding the difficult trip around the Peloponnesos. The city's heyday was in the 600s and early 500s BC, after which it was eclipsed by Athens.

Cult: in ancient Greece, the worship of a deity or local hero through such observances as animal sacrifices, libations, vows, and the dedication of gifts. Such worship typically took place outdoors.

Dark Age: term for the roughly 200-year period in Greek history that followed the final collapse of the Mycenaean civilization in the 12th century BC. Written documents are lacking for the period due to illiteracy; archaeological evidence suggests that it was a time of poverty, warfare, and limited communication.

Demeter: goddess of corn and fertility, patroness of agriculture, sister of Zeus, and mother of Persephone. The town of Eleusis, near Athens, was her cult center.

Democracy: "power of the people"; the form of government originated by Athens in which political institutions were open to all male citizens rather than being controlled by the wealthy few; a more limited concept than in modern times.

Dionysos: popular god of wine and intoxication; he was regarded as a bringer of joy but was also associated with death. During the Classical Age Dionysos was normally portrayed as a bearded man; later he was more often shown as an effeminate youth. His followers engaged in licentious revelry during his festivals.

Drachma: Greek silver coin; its name derives from the word for "handful," referring to the six smaller coins (obols) that were the equivalent of one drachma. Two- and four-drachma pieces were common; other denominations, such as half- and 12-drachma pieces, were also minted.

Ekklesia: the official assembly of adult male citizens in a Greek state. In democratic Athens, the ekklesia was the sovereign governing body. Any male citizen over the age of 18 could participate regardless of economic or social status. By the fourth century BC the ekklesia met in regular session 40 times a year to debate and vote on legislative proposals, military and administrative appointments, foreign policy, and judicial sentences. Meetings typically lasted for a couple of hours; votes were generally taken by a show of hands.

Entablature: architectural term for all the parts of a building above the columns, excluding the roof.

Etruria: region of central Italy inhabited by the Etruscans, a powerful pre-Roman people whose contact with Greek traders and colonists helped disseminate Greek culture and religion in Italy.

Grammatistes: a male instructor who taught reading, writing, arithmetic, and literature, especially Homeric poetry, to elementary-level students. Such teachers were poorly paid and not highly regarded.

Greaves: fabric- or leather-lined bronze leg guards worn by hoplites. Initially they only covered the lower leg; later types came up over the knee and were often molded to imitate the shape of calf muscles.

Gymnasium: a sports complex, normally municipally run, that also functioned as an important social and educational center in classical Greece. The facilities found at a gymnasium might include a covered running track, a colonnaded wrestling ground, fields for javelin and discus throwing, rooms for lectures and ball games, and bathing and oiling rooms for the athletes. Male citizens of all ages frequented the gymnasium, which derived its name from the Greek word *gymnos,* meaning naked.

Hades: Greek god of the underworld, brother to Zeus and Poseidon and husband of Persephone. Hades did not have a cult following, and, aside from the Persephone story, was not a major subject of myth. He was often referred to indirectly or euphemistically, as were other gods associated with death.

Hephaistos: god of fire and crafts, husband of Aphrodite; he was also associated with volcanoes. According to Athenian lore, he was the father of the Athenians' mythical original ancestor, Erichthonius.

Hera: the queen of the gods, Zeus's wife and sister, the patroness of women and protectress of cities. While her regal aspect was often stressed in art, in literature she frequently appeared as the jealous wife seeking vengeance on Zeus's paramours and their offspring by him.

Herakles: the most popular Greek hero, who came to be worshiped as a god; the Romans called him Hercules. Among the best known of the many myths surrounding Herakles were those describing his 12 labors. For one of these tasks, Herakles killed the Nemean lion by choking it, then used its own claws to scrape off its otherwise invulnerable skin, which he subsequently wore for its protective power.

Hermes: Zeus's son, the messenger of the gods, and the kindly but mischievous god of trade and travel. He was frequently pictured as a herald or traveler, with winged sandals, a wide-brimmed felt hat, or a herald's staff. Thieves, merchants, athletes, and shepherds came under his patronage.

Heroes/heroines: mythical or historical personages who stood apart from the common run of men by virtue of their exceptional strength, courage, beauty, or ability; many were the focus of cults. The epic poems feature heroes who were believed to have had a god as a parent or ancestor. Hero shrines were generally smaller than those of gods and were often built around ancient tombs; most hero-cults were very localized.

Hestia: the virgin goddess of the hearth and Zeus's sister, represented in art as a heavily veiled and draped maiden. Her name was uttered first in prayers; Greek settlers carried fire from the hearth dedicated to Hestia in their mother city's main public building to their new colonies.

Hetaira: literally, "companion"; euphemistic term for courtesans. Hetairai were distinguished from common prostitutes by their musical and conversational skills, education, and elegance.

Hoplites: heavily armed Greek infantrymen who marched and fought in close ranks *(see phalanx, below);* most recruits were middle-class citizens who could not afford to maintain a horse but could bear the cost of the hoplite's expensive armor and weapons.

Ionia: area along the central west coast of Asia Minor (including nearby islands) colonized by settlers from mainland Greece from about 1000 BC. Ionian Greeks, including Homer, played a central role in the early development of Greek history, philosophy, and literature following the Dark Age.

Kaloskagathos: a term of praise conveying that the man so described was brave, upstanding, attractive, and of good parentage, education, and upbringing.

Krater: a deep, widemouthed bronze or pottery bowl for mixing wine and water, normally a foot or a foot-and-a-half high. In art it is shown standing on the floor next to the couches on which drinkers reclined; the diluted wine was ladled from the krater into drinking cups by attractive young slaves.

Kylix: a wide, shallow drinking cup with two horizontal handles, suited for use by reclining banqueters.

Libation: a ritual pouring of a liquid on an altar or the ground to honor or propitiate gods, heroes, or the dead; wine, water, milk, oil, or honey were used.

Liturgy: "work for the people"; a public service that wealthy Athenians were required to provide at their own expense. The trierarchy *(see below)* was one type of liturgy; other liturgies were associated with festivals. Those subject to such duties would underwrite the cost of banquets, embassies to foreign festivals, theatrical performances, and the like.

Logographos: in Athens, a professional writer hired to compose speeches for litigants to deliver during trials. Both the accused and the accuser spoke for themselves before the court.

Metic: "dweller among"; Greek term for nonslave resident aliens. Many metics were Greeks who had emigrated from another Greek community. In Athens, metics were not allowed to participate in politics, marry citizens, or own property in Attica, even though they were subject to a special annual poll tax, liturgies, and military service. Metic status did confer commercial privileges and full civil rights.

Nike: the goddess of victory in military or athletic contests, characteristically depicted with wings. Images of Nike often adorned coins, vases, and the roofs of temples.

Oikos: the household, the basic unit of ancient Greek society; the term encompassed not only the house and the nuclear family inhabiting it but also dependent relatives, slaves, and freedmen and women, as well as the attached animals, land, and property.

Oligarchy: "leadership of the few"; a form of government in which the full exercise of political rights and power in a city-state was limited to the affluent, many but not necessarily all of whom were aristocrats. In the fifth century BC, Sparta was the leading proponent of oligarchy.

Olympian gods: the most important gods of the Greek pantheon, who were believed by Greeks to inhabit Mount Olympus. As represented in the Parthenon frieze, the 12 Olympians were Zeus, Hera, Poseidon, Athena, Apollo, Artemis, Aphrodite, Hermes, Demeter, Dionysos, Hephaistos, and Ares. Other gods, such as Hestia and Hades, were sometimes described as Olympians.

Ostracism: procedure used by the Athenian assembly in the fifth century BC to banish an unpopular or potentially dangerous citizen for 10 years, without revoking his citizenship or property rights. The assembly voted each winter on whether to hold an ostracism; if approved, a meeting was held in the Agora in a subsequent month. Each voter wrote the name of the individual he wanted exiled on a potsherd *(ostrakon),* which he then placed in an urn. If more than 6,000 votes were cast against one man, the individual so ostracized was forced to depart Attica within 10 days. An alternative explanation of the process of ostracism holds that the man who received the most votes was ostracized, provided that a total of at least 6,000 votes had been cast.

Ostrakon: a clay potsherd used for writing. Most ostraka found in Athens were used as tablets for inscribing the names of candidates for ostracism; elsewhere in the Greek world, receipts, lists, schoolwork, and letters have been found penned or incised on ostraka.

Paean: a hymn directed to a god, especially a healing god such as Apollo or Asklepios; typically sung at a religious festival or symposium, before a military action, or during an outbreak of illness or plague.

Paidagogos: "child leader"; a trusted household slave charged with escorting boys to school and supervising them while there; he also helped see to their upbringing at home.

Palaistra: a wrestling court, normally privately owned, where boys learned wrestling, boxing, and gymnastics. The wrestling ground itself was framed by a rectangular colonnade leading to changing rooms and washrooms. The palaistra was typically a smaller structure than a gymnasium, although it had a similar layout and might be incorporated into a gymnasium.

Panhellenic: relating to or involving all the Greek world. "Hellenes"—meaning men of Greece (Hellas)—was the name by which the ancient Greeks referred to themselves. The term applied not just to the natives of the Greek mainland and the surrounding islands but to the Greeks living in the city-states of Asia Minor and in the colonies.

Pediment: the triangular gable beneath a pitched roof; those at either end of a Greek temple were often decorated with painted sculptures.

Peplos: the traditional garment of Greek women; a sleeveless, typically ankle-length tunic formed from a single squarish piece of wool. The peplos was generally worn pinned at the shoulders and belted.

Phalanx: term for the battle formation of Greek hoplites; also applied to the battle order of Macedonian heavy infantry developed by Philip and his son, Alexander the Great. The Greek phalanx consisted of tightly packed rows of hoplites, typically eight ranks deep. The formation was suited for fighting on level ground but did not work well in difficult terrain.

Plutarch: Greek biographer of the first to early second century AD. His *Parallel Lives* pairs comparative biographies of famous men of classical Greece and republican Rome.

Polemarch: originally the commander in chief of Athens's army; the polemarch later lost this function and became a judicial officer concerned with metics and other foreigners.

Polis: a self-governing city-state; the basic political unit of the Greek world. The polis comprised a city, with its acropolis and agora, and the surrounding territory. There were several hundred such city-states in the Classical Age, each with its own laws, religious holidays, and coinage. The standard organs of government found in most city-states were the council, the assembly, and the magistracy, all of which were based in the city; the form of government varied over time and from polis to polis, but in the fifth century BC the two predominant types were oligarchies and democracies. The era of the independent polis ended with Alexander the Great.

Poseidon: god of the sea and earthquakes, brother of Zeus and Hades, and the tamer of horses. Athenians regarded the eighth day of the month as sacred to Poseidon.

Propylaia: a monumental roofed gateway to a sanctuary, notably that situated on the Acropolis in Athens.

Rhapsode: "song stitcher"; a professional reciter of Homeric and other epic poetry.

Sicily: the Mediterranean's largest island, colonized from the eighth century BC by Greeks and Carthaginians who frequently warred with each other or the island's native peoples. Much of Greek Sicily was ruled by tyrants *(see below)* during the fifth century BC, the most powerful being those of Syracuse.

Stoa: typically, a long, freestanding roofed building, rectangular in shape and single storied, with an open colonnade along one side and, occasionally, rooms behind the walled side. Stoas were located close to temples, gymnasia, or agoras, offering venues for public and private meetings, lectures, and dinners.

Strategos: a political and military leader. In addition to commanding land and naval forces, Athens's 10 annually elected and coequal strategoi supervised enlistment and the administration of the trierarch system *(see below)*. They had considerable influence in the political sphere as well.

Symposium: from the word for "drinking together"; an after-dinner drinking party attended by elite males. According to the protocol of a symposium, garlanded guests reclined on their left elbows, commonly two to a couch, and sang poems, posed riddles, played drinking games, and delivered philosophical speeches at the behest of a master of ceremonies designated by the group. Other entertainment was provided by musicians, jugglers, acrobats, and courtesans; hired performers and slaves of both sexes were also often required to provide sexual services to the symposiasts.

Terra cotta: baked clay; commonly used to fabricate such items as roof tiles, figurines, household vessels, and sarcophagi (coffins).

Theseus: legendary national hero and early king of Athens, raised by his mother in the Peloponnesos, credited in myth with killing the Cretan Minotaur and unifying all of Attica under the rule of Athens.

Thessaly: fertile region in northeastern Greece bounded by mountains, the most famous of which was Mount Olympus, the legendary home of the major gods of the Greek pantheon. Thessaly was dominated during most of the Classical Age by its landed aristocracy; it was considered culturally backward.

Thetes: the lowest class of free men in a Greek state, made up of day laborers and poor peasants.

Tholos: a circular building; most documented examples had a round roof resting on pillars. The tholos at Athens included a kitchen annex, where dinner was prepared at public expense for the council members on duty there.

Thracian: a member of one of the non-Greek tribes inhabiting Thrace, the region extending from northernmost Greece into modern-day Bulgaria and European Turkey. Greeks colonized its Aegean coastline from the eighth century BC. Fighting between the Thracian tribes of the interior provided a supply of war captives to the slave markets of Greece, where the Thracians were regarded as a backward people.

Trierarch: a wealthy Athenian appointed to command and pay for the upkeep of a warship in fulfillment of a liturgy. The trierarch served for a one-year term.

Trireme: the standard Greek warship during the fifth century BC. It was long and narrow, shallow drafted, and equipped with a bronze-clad ram on its prow. In battle the trireme was powered by three banks of rowers, each with his own oar. Larger warships accommodating several rowers at each oar began replacing the trireme in the fourth century BC.

Tyrant: term for a new type of monarch that first appeared in various Greek states in the seventh century BC; applied to unconstitutional rulers who took advantage of popular discontent with aristocratic governments by seizing power rather than achieving it through election or heredity. The term acquired negative connotations because of the dictatorial manner in which many tyrants ruled. Few tyrants succeeded in establishing multigenerational dynasties; some even helped pave the way for democracy by curbing the political dominance of the aristocrats.

Zeus: the paramount god of the Greek pantheon, god of the sky and weather; regarded as the dispenser of justice and orderer of the universe. He was often shown with a scepter or thunderbolt.

PRONUNCIATION GUIDE

Achilles (eh-KIL-eez)
Aegean (i-JEE-ehn)
Aeschylus (ES-ki-lehs)
Aetolia (i-TOH-li-eh)
Agamemnon (AG-eh-MEM-non)
Alcaeus (al-SEE-ehs)
Alkmene (alk-MEE-nee)
Anaxagoras (AN-ak-SAG-oh-rehs)
Antipater (AN-ti-PAY-ter)
Apollodoros (eh-POL-eh-DOHR-os)
Areopagus (ar-i-OP-eh-gehs)
Arginoussai (AR-gi-NOO-seye)
Aristophanes (AR-is-TOF-eh-neez)
Aristotle (AR-is-tot'l)
Asklepios (as-KLEE-pi-os)
Aspasia (as-PAY-shi-eh)
Attica (AT-i-keh)
Boeotia (bee-OH-sheh)
Briseis (BRIH-see-is)
Bucephalas (byoo-SEF-eh-lehs)
Callicratidas (KEH-li-KRAH-ti-dehs)
Callimachus (keh-LIM-eh-kehs)
Cerberus (SER-behr-ehs)
Chalkis (KAHL-kees)
Crete (kreet)
Cyclades (SIK-leh-deez)
Cyclops (SEYE-klops)
Delphi (DEL-fee)
Demarete (DEM-eh-REET)
Demosthenes (di-MOS-theh-neez)
Diodorus Siculus (DEYE-oh-DOHR-ehs
SIK-yeh-lehs)
Diomedes (DEYE-eh-MEE-deez)
Draco (DRAY-koh)
Eleusis (i-LOO-sis)
Empusa (em-PYOO-seh)
Ephesus (EF-eh-sehs)

Epidaurus (EP-i-DAW-rehs)
Epirus (i-PEER-ehs)
Eratosthenes (ER-eh-TOS-theh-neez)
Erechtheion (er-ek-THAY-on)
Eretria (e-REE-tri-eh)
Euboea (yoo-BEE-eh)
Euphiletos (yoo-FIL-eh-tos)
Euripides (yoo-RIP-eh-deez)
Ganymede (GAN-eh-MEED)
Gaugamela (GAW-geh-MEH-leh)
Granicus (GRA-nih-kehs)
Halicarnassus (HAL-i-kahr-NAS-ehs)
Herodotus (hi-ROD-eh-tehs)
Hesiod (HEE-si-ehd)
Hippias (HIP-i-ehs)
Hippocrates (hi-POK-reh-teez)
Hipponium (hi-POHN-i-ehm)
Illyria (i-LEER-ee-eh)
Ionia (eye-OH-ni-eh)
Iphigeneia (if-i-jeh-NEYE-eh)
Issus (IS-ehs)
Kephalos (KEH-fa-los)
Kleisthenes (KLEYES-theh-neez)
Knossos (KNOS-os)
Laconia (leh-KOH-ni-eh)
Larissa (leh-RIS-eh)
Lamia (LAY-mee-eh)
Lesbos (LEZ-bos)
Lysias (LIS-i-ehs)
Macedonia (MAS-i-DOH-ni-eh)
Megara (MEG-eh-reh)
Menelaus (MEN-eh-LAY-ehs)
Mikion (mi-KEE-on)
Miletus (meye-LEE-tehs)
Miltiades (mil-TEYE-eh-deez)
Mycenae (meye-SEE-nee)
Mytilene (mit'l-EE-nee)

Nemea (NEE-mee-eh)
Odysseus (oh-DIS-ee-ehs)
Olynthus (oh-LIN-thuhs)
Panathenaic (PAN-ath-eh-NAY-ik)
Pasion (PAH-see-on)
Patroklos (peh-TRO-klos)
Pausanias (paw-SAY-ni-ehs)
Peisistratus (peye-SIS-treh-tehs)
Peloponnesos (PEL-oh-peh-NEE-sos)
Pericles (PER-i-kleez)
Persephone (pehr-SEF-oh-ni)
Phidias (FID-ee-ehs)
Piraeus (peye-REE-ehs)
Plataea (pleh-TEE-eh)
Plato (PLAY-toh)
Plutarch (PLOO-tahrk)
Pnyx (p'niks)
Polyphemos (POL-ee-FEE-mos)
Salamis (SAL-eh-mis)
Samos (SAY-mos)
Sappho (SAF-oh)
Semele (SEM-eh-LEE)
Socrates (SOK-reh-teez)
Sogdiana (SOG-dee-AN-eh)
Solon (SOH-lon)
Sophocles (SOF-oh-kleez)
Tenedos (TEN-eh-dos)
Thargelia (thahr-GAY-lee-eh)
Thebes (theebz)
Themistokles (thi-MIS-toh-kleez)
Thermopylae (thehr-MOP-eh-lee)
Theseus (THEE-see-ehs)
Thrasybulus (thras-IB-yoo-lehs)
Thucydides (thoo-SID-i-deez)
Tyndareus (tin-DAIR-EE-ehs)
Xanthippos (zan-THIP-os)
Xenophon (ZEN-oh-fon)

ACKNOWLEDGMENTS

The editors wish to thank the following individuals and institutions for their valuable assistance in the preparation of this volume:

F. W. Hamdorf, Staatliche Antikensammlungen und Glyptothek, Munich; Philip Kaplan, Department of Ancient History, University of Pennsylvania, Philadelphia, Pennsylvania; Ursula Kästner, Staatliche Museen zu Berlin—Preussischer Kulturbesitz, Antikenmuseum, Berlin; Heidrun Klein, Bildarchiv Preussischer Kulturbesitz, Berlin; Manfred Korfmann, Institut für Ur-und Frühgeschichte, Universität Tübingen, Tübingen, Germany; Norbert Kunisch, Kunstsammlungen der Ruhr-Universität Bochum, Bochum, Germany; Michael Maass, Badisches Museum Karlsruhe, Karlsruhe, Germany; Marie Montembault, Département des Antiquités Grecques et Romaines, Musée du Louvre, Paris; Ori Z. Soltes, B'nai B'rith Klutznick National Jewish Museum, Washington, D.C.

BIBLIOGRAPHY

BOOKS

Adkins, Lesley, and Roy A. Adkins. *Handbook to Life in Ancient Greece.* New York: Facts On File, 1997.

Amos, H. D., and A. G. P. Lang. *These Were the Greeks.* Chester Springs, Pa.: Dufour Editions, 1982.

Andronicus, Manolis. *Delphi.* Athens: Ekdotike Athenon S.A., 1982.

Archibald, Zofia. *Discovering the World of the Ancient Greeks.* New York: Facts On File, 1991.

Atlas of Classical Archaeology. Ed. by M. I. Finley. New York: McGraw-Hill, 1977.

Barber, Elizabeth Wayland. *Women's Work: The First 20,000 Years.* New York: W. W. Norton & Co., 1994.

Barber, Robin. *Greece.* London: A. & C. Black, 1988.

Barron, John. *Greek Sculpture.* New York: E. P. Dutton and Co., 1965.

Barrow, Robin. *Greek and Roman Education* (Inside the Ancient World series). London: Bristol Classical Press, 1996.

Boardman, John. *The Parthenon and Its Sculptures.* Austin: University of Texas Press, 1985.

Bowra, C. M., and the Editors of Time-Life Books. *Classical Greece* (Great Ages of Man series). New York: Time-Life Books, 1965.

Briers, Audrey. *Sporting Success in Ancient Greece and Rome.* Oxford: Ashmolean Museum, 1994.

Burkert, Walter. *Greek Religion.* Cambridge, Mass.: Harvard University Press, 1985.

Burn, Lucilla. *The British Museum Book of Greek and Roman Art.* New York: Thames and Hudson, 1991.

Bury, J. B., and Russell Meiggs. *A History of Greece: To the Death of Alexander the Great.* New York: St. Martin's Press, 1975.

Casson, Lionel. *Ships and Seafaring in Ancient Times.* London: British Museum Press, 1994.

Connolly, Peter. *Greek Armies.* London: Macdonald & Co., 1977.

Douskou, Iris. *Athens: The City and Its Museums.* Athens: Ekdotike Athenon S.A., 1986.

Fantham, Elaine, et al. *Women in the Classical World.* New York: Oxford University Press, 1994.

Flacelière, Robert. *Daily Life in Greece at the Time of Pericles.* Trans. by Peter Green. New York: Macmillan, 1965.

Fitzhardinge, L. F. *The Spartans.* London: Thames and Hudson, 1980.

Garland, Robert. *The Greek Way of Life: From Conception to Old Age.* Ithaca, N.Y.: Cornell University Press, 1990.

Grant, Michael. *A Guide to the Ancient World: A Dictionary of Classical Place Names.* Bronx, N.Y.: H. W. Wilson, 1986.

Greece: Temples, Tombs, and Treasures. Alexandria, Va.: Time-Life Books, 1994.

Green, Peter. *Ancient Greece: An Illustrated History.* New York: Thames and Hudson, 1979.

Haward, Anne. *Penelope to Poppaea* (Inside the Ancient World series). London: Bristol Classical Press, 1996.

Historical Atlas of the World. Maplewood, N.J.: Hammond, 1974.

Homer:
The Iliad. Trans. by Robert Fagles. New York: Penguin Books, 1990.
The Odyssey. Trans. by Robert Fagles. New York: Viking, 1996.

Howatson, M. C., and Ian Chilvers, eds. *The Concise Oxford Companion to Classical Literature.* Oxford: Oxford University Press, 1993.

Kebric, Robert. *Greek People.* Mountain View, Calif.: Mayfield Publishing, 1997.

Keuls, Eva C. *The Reign of the Phallus: Sexual Politics in Ancient Athens.* Berkeley: University of California Press, 1993.

Lacey, W. K. *Die Familie im Antiken Griechenland.* Trans. by Ute Winter. London: Thames and Hudson, 1983.

Levi, Peter:
Atlas of the Greek World. New York: Facts On File, 1980.
The Greek World (The Cultural Atlas of the World series). Alexandria, Va.: Stonehenge, 1990.

Ling, Roger. *The Greek World* (The Making of the Past series). New York: Peter Bedrick Books, 1988.

Loverance, Rowena. *Ancient Greece.* New York: Viking, 1993.

Martin, Thomas R. *Ancient Greece: From Prehistoric to Hellenistic Times.* New Haven, Conn.: Yale University Press, 1996.

Massey, Michael. *Women in Ancient Greece and Rome.* Cambridge: Cambridge University Press, 1988.

The Metropolitan Museum of Art: Greece and Rome. New York: Metropolitan Museum of Art, 1987.

Mikalson, Jon D. *Athenian Popular Religion.* Chapel Hill: University of North Carolina Press, 1989.

More, Daisy, and John Bowman. *Clash of East and West: The Persians, Imperial Greece* (Imperial Visions: The Rise and Fall of Empires series). New York: HBJ Press, 1980.

Morrison, J. S., and J. F. Coates. *The Athenian Trireme: The History and Reconstruction of an Ancient Greek Warship.* Cambridge: Cambridge University Press, 1986.

National Geographic Atlas of the World. Washington, D.C.: National Geographic Society, 1970.

Neils, Jenifer. *Goddess and Polis: The Panathenaic Festival in Ancient Athens.* Hanover, N.H.: Dartmouth College, 1992.

The Olympic Games: A Book of Records and Reminiscence. New York: Time-Life Books, 1967.

The Oxford Companion to Classical Literature. Ed. by M. C. Howatson. Oxford: Oxford University Press, 1989.

The Oxford Companion to Wine. Ed. by Jancis Robinson. Oxford: Oxford University Press, 1994.

The Oxford History of the Classical World. Ed. by John Boardman, Jasper Griffin, and Oswyn Murray. Oxford: Oxford University Press, 1986.

Parke, H. W. *Festivals of the Athenians.* Ithaca, N.Y.:

Cornell University Press, 1977.

Peach, Susan, and Anne Millard. *The Greeks.* London: Usborne Publishing, 1990.

Pearson, Anne. *Ancient Greece.* London: Dorling Kindersley, 1992.

Pedley, John Griffiths. *Greek Art and Archaeology.* New York: Harry N. Abrams, 1993.

Poole, Lynn, and Gray Poole. *History of Ancient Olympic Games.* New York: Ivan Obolensky, 1963.

Powell, Anton. *Greece: 1600-30 BC.* New York: Franklin Watts, 1987.

Quennell, Marjorie, and Charles Henry Quennell. *Everyday Things in Ancient Greece.* London: B. T. Batsford, 1954.

Rodgers, William Ledyard. *Greek and Roman Naval Warfare: A Study of Strategy, Tactics, and Ship Design from Salamis (480 B.C.) to Actium (31 B.C.).* Annapolis, Md.: Naval Institute Press, 1964.

Sacks, David. *Encyclopedia of the Ancient Greek World.* New York: Facts On File, 1995.

The Search: An Exhibition. Boston: New York Graphic Society, 1980.

A Soaring Spirit (TimeFrame series). Alexandria, Va.: Time-Life Books, 1987.

Swaddling, Judith. *The Ancient Olympic Games.* London: British Museum Press, 1980.

The Times Atlas of World History. Ed. by Geoffrey Barraclough (4th ed., ed. by Geoffrey Parker). London: Times Books, 1993.

Williams, Dyfri, and Jack Ogden. *Greek Gold: Jewelry of the Classical World.* New York: Harry N. Abrams, 1994.

Windrow, Martin. *The Greek Hoplite* (The Soldier through the Ages series). London: Franklin Watts, 1985.

The World of Athens: An Introduction to Classical Athenian Culture. Cambridge: Cambridge University Press, 1984.

Zaidman, Louise B., and Pauline S. Pantel. *Religion in the Ancient Greek City.* Cambridge: Cambridge University Press, 1995.

PERIODICALS

Archaeology, July/August 1996.

PICTURE CREDITS

INDEX

Numerals in italics indicate an illustration of the subject mentioned.

Time-Life Books is a division of Time Life Inc.

TIME LIFE INC.
PRESIDENT and CEO: George Artandi

TIME-LIFE BOOKS
PRESIDENT: Stephen R. Frary
PUBLISHER/MANAGING EDITOR: Neil Kagan

What Life Was Like
AT THE DAWN OF DEMOCRACY

EDITOR: Denise Dersin
DIRECTOR, NEW PRODUCT DEVELOPMENT:
Elizabeth D. Ward
MARKETING DIRECTORS: Pamela R. Farrell,
Joseph A. Kuna

Deputy Editor: Paula York-Soderlund
Design Director: Cynthia T. Richardson
Text Editor: Robin Currie
Associate Editors/Research and Writing:
Trudy W. Pearson, Jarelle S. Stein
Senior Copyeditors: Anne Farr, Mary Beth Oelkers-Keegan
Technical Art Specialist: John Drummond
Picture Coordinator: David Herod
Editorial Assistant: Christine Higgins

Special Contributors: Anthony Allan, Ronald H. Bailey, Dónal Kevin Gordon (chapter text); Gaye Brown, Ann Lee Bruen, Mark Galan, Stacy W. Hoffhaus, Jacqueline L. Shaffer, Marilyn Murphy Terrell, Elizabeth Thompson, Myrna Traylor-Herndon (research-writing); Magdalena Anders, Kristin A. Dittman, Ann-Louise Gates, Beth Levin, Patricia Nelson (research); James Michael Lynch (editing); Barbara L. Klein (index); Fred Holz (art).

Correspondents: Maria Vincenza Aloisi (Paris), Christine Hinze (London), Christina Lieberman (New York). Valuable assistance was also provided by: Kalypso Gordon (Athens), Elisabeth Kraemer-Singh, Angelika Lemmer (Bonn).

Director of Finance: Christopher Hearing
Director of Book Production: Marjann Caldwell
Director of Publishing Technology: Betsi McGrath
Director of Photography and Research: John Conrad Weiser
Director of Editorial Administration: Barbara Levitt
Production Manager: Gertraude Schaefer
Quality Assurance Manager: James King
Chief Librarian: Louise D. Forstall

Consultant:
Jeremy McInerney is an assistant professor in the Department of Classical Studies at the University of Pennsylvania. He has taught both undergraduate and graduate courses at Penn, ranging from the history of ancient Greece to Greek epigraphy. Dr. McInerney received graduate degrees from the University of California, Berkeley, and has published articles on a variety of topics in Greek history and archaeology. He is currently completing a book on the history of the region around Delphi from the Bronze Age to Roman times.

Library of Congress Cataloging-in-Publication Data
What life was like at the dawn of democracy: classical
Athens, 525-322 BC/by the Editors of Time-Life Books.
    p. cm.
    Includes bibliographical references and index.
    ISBN 0-7835-5453-2
    1. Athens (Greece)—Civilization 2. Greece—History—Athenian supremacy. 479-431 B.C. 3. Pericles, 499-429 B.C. I. Time-Life Books. II. Title: Classical Athens, 525-322 BC
DF227.W43 1997   97-39764
938'.5—DC21   CIP

Other Publications:
HISTORY
The American Story
Voices of the Civil War
The American Indians
Lost Civilizations
Mysteries of the Unknown
Time Frame
The Civil War
Cultural Atlas

COOKING
Weight Watchers® Smart Choice Recipe Collection
Great Taste~Low Fat
Williams-Sonoma Kitchen Library

SCIENCE/NATURE
Voyage Through the Universe

DO IT YOURSELF
The Time-Life Complete Gardener
Home Repair and Improvement
The Art of Woodworking
Fix It Yourself

TIME-LIFE KIDS
Library of First Questions and Answers
A Child's First Library of Learning
I Love Math
Nature Company Discoveries
Understanding Science & Nature

For information on and a full description of any of the Time-Life Books series listed above, please call 1-800-621-7026 or write:

Reader Information
Time-Life Customer Service
P.O. Box C-32068
Richmond, Virginia 23261-2068

This volume is one in a series on world history that uses contemporary art, artifacts, and personal accounts to create an intimate portrait of daily life in the past.

Other volumes included in the
What Life Was Like series:

On the Banks of the Nile: Egypt, 3050-30 BC
In the Age of Chivalry: Medieval Europe, AD 800-1500
When Rome Ruled the World: The Roman Empire, 100 BC- AD 200
When Longships Sailed: Vikings, AD 800-1100